TWAYNE'S WORLD AUTHORS SERIES
A Survey of the World's Literature

Sylvia E. Bowman, Indiana University
GENERAL EDITOR

GREECE

Mary P. Gianos, Detroit Institute of Technology
EDITOR

Anna Comnena

(TWAS 213)

TWAYNE'S WORLD AUTHORS SERIES (TWAS)

The purpose of TWAS is to survey the major writers —novelists, dramatists, historians, poets, philosophers, and critics—of the nations of the world. Among the national literatures covered are those of Australia, Canada, China, Eastern Europe, France, Germany, Greece, India, Italy, Japan, Latin America, the Netherlands, New Zealand, Poland, Russia, Scandinavia, Spain, and the African nations, as well as Hebrew, Yiddish, and Latin Classical literatures. This survey is complemented by Twayne's United States Authors Series and English Authors Series.

The intent of each volume in these series is to present a critical-analytical study of the works of the writer; to include biographical and historical material that may be necessary for understanding, appreciation, and critical appraisal of the writer; and to present all material in clear, concise English—but not to vitiate the scholarly content of the work by doing so.

Anna Comnena

By RAE DALVEN
Ladycliff College

Twayne Publishers, Inc.   ::   New York

To the Memory of my Mother

Anna Comnena

Anna Comnena in her Alexiad's prologue,
laments her widowhood.

Her soul is in a dizzy state. "And I
wet my eyes," she tells us, "with rivulets
of tears . . . Alas for the waves" in her life,
"Alas for the revolutions." Pain burns her
"to her bones and her marrow and the cleaving of her soul."

More like the truth, however, is that this ambitious woman
knew only one mortal sorrow;
she had only one deep longing
(though she never admits it), this haughty Greek woman,
that she was never able, with all her dexterity,
to acquire the Kingship; it was snatched
almost out of her hands by the impertinent John.

                                                          1920.

Foreword

Anna Comnena was no doubt the most educated woman the medieval Greek world produced. She knew the Greek classics, particularly Homer, well, and her knowledge of medicine rivaled that of the most prominent physicians of the period. But what commends her to the modern historian is her work as a historian herself. *The Alexiad,* as her history of the reign of her father is known, is one of the two most original works of Byzantine historiography.

In the pages which follow, Dr. Rae Dalven has brought together in an incisive narrative all the salient elements of Anna's life, Anna as a child, as a daughter, as a wife, as a woman of ambition, and of course also as a historian. But Anna's life was so intertwined with that of her family that Dalven's book is also a history of the early Comneni, one of the most brilliant families of the Byzantine Empire. Dr. Dalven has aimed her book at the general reader, but there are points in it that should prove useful to scholars. It should stimulate interest in the history and civilization of the Byzantine Empire.

PETER CHARANIS

Voorhees Professor of History
Rutgers University

Preface

The *Alexiad,* modeled after Homer's *Iliad,* and composed in fifteen books, is the history of Emperor Alexios I Comnenos, written by his firstborn child, Anna Comnena, in 1148. Except for a ten-line poem to the Logos,[1] two of her seals which have come down to us,[2] and a four-page Prologue to her Will,[3] the *Alexiad* is the only other work that Anna wrote which can help a biographer to know this remarkable but star-crossed Byzantine princess as a historian and as a woman.

Fate seemed dead-set against bringing the *Alexiad* out of its obscurity; four centuries elapsed before Anna's history of her father's reign came to the attention of the world. From the Latin dissertation by Joh. Conradi Fueslini, published in Thuringia in 1766, we learn that a man named Thaunus mentioned the *Alexiad* in his History in 1223, and stated that this was an invaluable work which should go down to posterity.[4]

From both the Fueslini dissertation, and a study made by Leib of the existing manuscripts and the text of the *Alexiad,* we learn that in 1590, a well-known erudite scholar named Pierre du Faur de Saint-Jorri came in contact with Jacques Cujas, possessor of a manuscript of the *Alexiad,* but the death of the former in 1600, and the disappearance of the latter, left no traces of the manuscript.[5] From a manuscript at the Library of Augsburg, we learn that in 1610 the *Alexiad* was sold at Munich to David Hoeschel, who abridged it into eight books and had it published in 1618, although the dedication bears the date 1610.[6] This was the first knowledge the world had of the existence of the *Alexiad,* and it served to awaken the curiosity of the public. Fueslini states that in the Hoeschel edition the name of Pierre du Faur appears in the dedication and that Cujas entrusted his manuscript to him, although he asked him not to have it published.[7] In 1649, Chancellor Seguir, a man of letters, persuaded Pierre Poussines, a theologian who had a love for Byzantine letters, to translate Anna's history, which he did with the assistance of the Archbishop of Toulouse, Charles de Monthal. In this hybrid copy of the *Alexiad,* which consists of a Latin translation and a glossary, Poussines calls Anna "The Tenth Muse" and "Pallas of Byzantine Greece."[8] This edition is preserved at the College of Jesuits at Toulouse. In 1672 a Schopen edition of the *Alexiad* appeared at Bonn with a new Latin translation and the Greek text.[9] Leib states that a twelfth-century manuscript found at Florence served as the basis for the edition of A. Reifferscheid, published in two volumes in Leipzig in 1884.[10] Dr. Elizabeth Dawes used the Reifferscheid publication for her English translation of the *Alexiad,* which first appeared in London in 1928 and was reprinted in 1967.

The Greek text of the *Alexiad* used in this study is included in Bernard Leib's three-volume French translation of the *Alexiade,* published in Paris by the Société d'Edition "Les Belles Lettres" from 1937 to 1945. Quotations from the *Alexiad* are taken from the English translation by Elizabeth A. S. Dawes, first published in 1928 by Kegan, Paul, Trench Trubner and Co., and reprinted in 1967 by Routledge and Kegan Paul, Ltd. I used the Greek text of *Hyle Historias* by Nicephoros Bryennios found in *Migne Patrologia Graeca,* Volume 127, pp. 23-215. I have also used "Les Quatres Livres des Histoires," the French translation of Bryennios's *Hyle Historias* by Henri Grégoire.

RAE DALVEN

Ladycliff College

Acknowledgments

I wish to acknowledge my thanks to Professor Mary P. Gianos, editor of the Greek Series of Twayne's World Authors Series, for her guidance in the format of this book. I am especially grateful to Professor Peter Charanis, for reading my manuscript and making some valuable suggestions. To my friend Procope S. Costas, Professor of Classics at Brooklyn College, I offer thanks for translating several passages of Byzantine Greek, also for his many helpful suggestions about authorities in an area of Greek letters which was unfamiliar to me before I began this study. I also wish to thank Dr. Basil Vlavianos for reading my manuscript and especially Mr. William Pappas for making some helpful suggestions. I am indebted to Professor Leandros Vranousis and Professor George A. Papademetriou, both of the Academy of Athens, who graciously allowed me to use their Byzantine library when I was in Athens, and helped generally to deepen my understanding of this interesting period in Greek civilization. To the late Sister Catherine Frederick, chief librarian at Ladycliff, goes a special vote of thanks for repeatedly procuring for me, through the interloan library, books which I would not otherwise have obtained easily. I am also grateful to the librarians at Dumbarton Oaks Library for letting me use their library, as well as to Mr. Miles M. Jefferson of the Reference Room at the New York Public Library at Forty-Second Street in New York for helping me to locate books more easily. I am most grateful to Sister Mary Immaculata, Latin teacher at the Ladycliff Academy, for her translation into English of a Latin dissertation of use in this study. Lastly, I wish to thank Routledge and Kegan Paul, Ltd., for granting me permission to quote from the *Alexiad*, translated by Elizabeth A. S. Dawes.

Contents

Chronology

1056   Birth of Alexios Comnenos.

1057   September 2: Isaac Comnenos, uncle of Alexios, is crowned emperor in Hagia Sophia by Patriarch Michael Cerularios.

1059   November 22: Emperor Isaac Comnenos abdicates.

1066   Birth of Irene Ducas, daughter of Maria of Bulgaria[1] and Andronicos Ducas, and mother of Anna Comnena.

1067   John Comnenos, father of Alexios, dies.

1070   Death of Manuel Comnenos, brother of Alexios.

1074   Birth of Constantine Ducas, Anna Comnena's first fiancé.

1077   October 14: Death of Andronicos Ducas, Irene's father.

1078   January (?): Marriage of Alexios Comnenos to Irene Ducas.

1081   February 14: Alexios and his brother Isaac flee during the night of the Sunday of Quinquagesima, or "Cheese-eating Sunday."

1081   April 1: Alexios Comnenos crowned emperor of Byzantium in Hagia Sophia, with Constantine Ducas as coregent. Irene is crowned seven days later.

1081   Birth of Nicephoros Bryennios, future husband of Anna Comnena.

1083   December 2: Birth of Anna Comnena, Porphyrogenete,[2] acclaimed successor to the throne.

1085   Birth of Anna's sister Maria Porphyrogenete.

1087   Birth of Anna's brother John Porphyrogenitos, future emperor of the Byzantine Empire.

1092   John Porphyrogenitos proclaimed basileus. Anna loses her rights to succession.

1092   Birth of Anna's sister Eudocia Porphyrogenete.

1095   Birth of Theodora Porphyrogenete, Anna Comnena's sister.

1095   Death of Constantine Ducas, Anna's first fiancé.

1097   Anna Comnena is married to Nicephoros Bryennios.

1098   A first son is born to Anna and Nicephoros and named Alexios.

1100   Anna Dalassena, Mother of the Comneni, retires to the monastery Pantepoptes. A second son is born to Anna and Nicephoros and named John. A daughter named Irene Ducas is born to Anna and Nicephoros. Another daughter is born to Anna and Nicephoros. Her name is not mentioned anywhere.

1103   John Porphyrogenitos marries Princess Prisca of Hungary, daughter of Saint Ladislas, prince of the Abasgi.

1104   Twins are born to John Porphyrogenitos and Princess Prisca, a boy and a girl.

1105   Anna Dalassena dies.

1105   Adrian Comnenos, brother of Alexios, dies.

1106   (?) Death of Isaac Comnenos, brother of Alexios.[3]

1114   Anna joins her father and mother at Philippopolis.

1118   August 15: Death of Alexios I. His son John II becomes emperor of Byzantium. John's wife assumes the name of Irene at his ascension.

1121   Empress Irene writes her *Typikon* for the monastery Kecharitomene.

1129   Andronicos Comnenos, brother of Anna Comnena, is killed in battle with the Turks.

1133   February 19: Death of Empress Irene at the age of sixty-seven.[4]

1134   August 13: Death of Empress Irene Prisca, wife of John II.

1138   Death of Nicephoros Bryennios.

1138   Death of Theodora, wife of John Ducas Bryennios.

1143   Death of Emperor John II.

1148   Anna Comnena completes her *Alexiad.*

1153-   Death of Anna Comnena.[5]
1155(?)

CHAPTER 1

The State of Byzantium 1025-1081

For the preceding Emperors had been very inefficient in all military and warlike matters and had thus driven the State of Rome in very dire straits. (*Alexiad*, III, 9, p. 90)

ANNA Comnena, first woman historian, wrote her *Alexiad*, as she states in her Preface, to recount the achievements of her father, Emperor Alexios I (1081-1118), so that they would not be lost in silence. As the most learned and cultured woman of her age and as a woman of letters, Anna must surely have been familiar with the state of Byzantium when her father ascended the throne. All Byzantine historians agree that Anna's statement quoted above is no exaggeration. As one Byzantine authority noted, "For the most part control during the years 1025-81 lay with rulers who were not competent to deal with military matters."[1]

On the death of Basil II in 1025, the Byzantine Empire had reached the apogee of its glory. A historical map of that year shows that its frontiers extended from the Danube to Syria, and from the Tigris to the Euphrates rivers. Armenia had been annexed as far as Azerbaijan; Antioch, Bulgaria, the islands of Crete and Cyprus, and a third of Italy, including Calabria and Apulia, were well within the Byzantine orbit.[2] Constantinople was reputed to be the most brilliant center of European civilization; Byzantium was mistress of the whole Balkan peninsula; the treasury had a reserve of 220,000,000 francs.[3]

Anna finds it hard to define the former width of the empire. She would have us believe that at the height of its glory the Byzantine Empire included "Egypt, Meroë, all the Troglodyte country and the region adjacent to the Torrid zone, and in the other direction far-famed Thule, and the races who dwell in the northern lands and over whose heads the North Pole stands." Anna is carried away here, probably to focus more sharply on the state of the Byzantine Empire when her father ascended the

17

throne. "In these later times," she reflects mournfully, "the boundary of the Roman rule was the neighboring Bosporus on the east and the city of Adrianople on the west" (VI, 11, p. 159). Her father would have to use all his talents to recapture even a fraction of their earlier Byzantine glory.

Anna does not always give the reader the specific causes of the disastrous decline of Byzantium during the fifty-six years which preceded her father's reign. One reason for her omission of some of these facts is that she knew other contemporary historians had dealt with these events; the reader could turn to the sources she herself had used. More important perhaps is the fact that Anna was eager to record the events of her father's reign, which covered a period of thirty-seven years. She had a good deal of ground to cover. Furthermore, as she states in the *Alexiad,* this is a history of "my father the Emperor." Nonetheless, we must know these causes if we are to comprehend the enormous difficulties which confronted Alexios when he ascended the throne in 1081.

All through the eleventh century, Byzantium was menaced by three external foreign invaders on at least three frontiers: the Patzinaks (Anna also calls them Scythians by their classical name) from the north, the Normans from the west, and the Seljuk Turks from the east. The Cumans (also known as Kipchaks and Polovtsi), a Turkish people who dwelt north of the Patzinaks, and the Uzes, another nomadic people of Turkish origin, were less frequent invaders.

The Patzinaks (also known as Pechenegs), a people of the Ghuzz tribes, akin linguistically to the Turks, were the most dreaded of all the nomads. Anna knew the Patzinaks had been troubling the empire for several years; she mentions them only occasionally because, as she says, of the plethora of subjects she had to cover in her father's reign.

The Patzinaks had not always been enemies of Byzantium. In the tenth century the Byzantines used the Patzinaks as allies against their enemies of the north, the Bulgarians, Hungarians, and Russians, who were advancing southward.[4] The Patzinaks made incursions into Greek territory when they became the immediate neighbors of the Byzantine Empire. After Basil II annexed Bulgaria, there was no longer any buffer state between the Byzantine Empire and the Patzinaks beyond the Danube. The Patzinaks could now cross more easily into Greek territory.

Even then, they were allowed to settle on Greek soil and, as George Ostrogorsky observes, "by making a virtue of necessity, the newcomers were employed to garrison the frontier and used for military service."[5] As time went on, however, the Patzinaks exploited the weakness of the emperors who succeeded Basil II, and they ravaged the Byzantine countryside until Byzantium had to take up arms against them. From then on the Patzinaks never ceased to invade Byzantium. "There was virtually no reign," writes Peter Charanis, "from the accession of Constantine VIII in 1025 to the end of the eleventh century that did not witness some Pecheneg invasion of the territories of the Empire in the Balkan peninsula."[6]

The Seljuk Turks, also members of the Turkish tribe of Ghuzz, whom Anna refers to as "the godless Turks," invaded the Byzantine Empire from the east. They were the most frequent invaders. In the eleventh century, the Seljuks had subdued Persian lands, drove through Mesopotamia and captured Baghdad. Before long they took possession of the whole of the Near East up to the frontiers of Byzantium. Then they cast their eyes on Byzantium itself.[7]

The Normans, whom Anna also refers to as Franks, Celts, and Latins, were redoubtable warlike adventurers who made frequent emigrations for a variety of reasons. A group of forty Norman pilgrims first arrived at the siege of Salerno, which Frederick Chalandon places either at the end of 1015 or at the beginning of 1016.[8] Others followed, and before long they exploited the dissensions of the Muslims and the native princes. With cunning and cruelty, they soon carved out principalities for themselves. Anna, who was an eyewitness of the First Crusade, knew that the Normans had their eyes on the Byzantine throne. She admits that they were brave and daring warriors; she admires their looks; but to her they are the worst of all the barbarians who invaded the empire. She refers repeatedly to their unstable character, their greed for money, their oath-breaking, their covetousness.

It must be said, however, that these foreign invaders, attacking the Byzantine Empire on three frontiers, would not have progressed as far as they did had not Byzantium been torn by several internal conflicts. There was the constant two-way struggle between the civil aristocracy in the capital and the military magnates of Asia Minor, each of whom fought for domination over the affairs of the state. The civil aristocracy, essentially antimilitary, aimed at weakening the power of the central government. Basil II had been able to check the power of the wealthy military magnates of the provinces because of his control of the army, the treasury, and the rural economy, which was the lifeblood of the state. Furthermore, he succeeded in curbing the powerful (*dynatoi*), as the military magnates were called, by enforcing on them the *allelengyon,* a system which compelled the powerful to pay taxes of the small holder, or farmer in the village community. As one historian notes, "this class cultivated the land, provided for the general needs, paid the taxes, and furnished the army with recruits."[9]

When Basil II died, the *allelengyon* was either no longer enforced, or it was abolished, and the powerful refused to pay the tax for the poor. The small free peasant and soldier-farmers of the provinces who were unable to pay the tax were now forced either to migrate or to sell their land and their liberty to the powerful, who reduced them to the status of dependent tenants on a large estate. Deprived of their holdings and their freedom, the peasants of Asia Minor were unwilling to offer any resistance to the Turks. As the domains of the landed class increased, so much more did they escape the administrative control of the central authority. They also won important immunities which further diminished the resources of the state. Ecclesiastical estates were also granted privileges exempting their owners from taxes and public obligations.[10] "Little by little," writes Charles Diehl, "a great feudal aristocracy had grown up within the Empire,—especially in the Asiatic provinces,—possessed of vast domains, dependents, and vassals, whose influence was still further augmented by the high administrative offices ... and military commands which placed the army in its hands ... this nobility was a political as well as a social menace to the government."[11] The poor were overburdened with taxes and the central government was compelled to debase the coinage in order to have some fixed revenue; this undermined the Byzantine economy both within the state and in international trade. With the loss of recruits, the state was forced to hire mercenaries of all races, totally foreign to the country, devoid of all patriotism. The crammed treasury that Basil II had built was fast being depleted.

Probably the most significant factor which contributed to the success of the Turkish tribes was the constant foe-ally relation-

ship which the Greeks themselves fostered. Nicephoros Botaneiates had set a precedent by enrolling large numbers of Turks
under his standard and using them to garrison the towns he
took. "For the first time," writes Runciman, "Turkish hordes
found themselves inside the great cities of Western Anatolia.
They might be the mercenaries of the new Emperor; but he would
not find it easy to dislodge them."[12] The Scythians were allied
to the rebel Bryennios. Anna herself tells us that outside the
regular army of Bryennios, there were some "allied Scythians,
distinguished by barbaric weapons" (I, 5, p. 15). Turkish
soldiers were also among the troops of Alexios when he was
sent to capture Bryennios (I, 4, p. 14). Botaneiates secured the
help of the Turks to dethrone Michael VII. Just before Alexios
and Isaac Comnenos revolted for the Byzantine throne, Cyzicus
had been taken by the Turks. This did not prevent the Caesar
John Ducas from inviting a contingent of Turks to join in
the revolt (II, 6, p. 58). When Nicephoros Melissenos rebelled
against Nicephoros III, he gave up the possession of Nicaea to
Sulayman.[13] Again during the First Crusade, as Claude Cahen
notes, "the troops of the basileus were led by a commander of
Turkish origin in their effort to reconquer Anatolia from the
Turks."[14] And a Greek historian writes, "With the Turks, they
not only effected an agreement of compromise and gave them
many privileges, but they also made them allies and they invited
them to help when seditious movements broke out in Asia
Minor."[15]

The Turks were also aided in their advance into Byzantine
territory by the constant disagreements among Byzantine leaders
and by a lack of openness in their negotiations with the Turks.
The withdrawal of frontier troops to combat a civil war, to crush
a rebellion or the commonplace insurrections, were like many
invitations to the Turks to ravage the empire. Particularly
demoralizing was the diversity of the Byzantine forces made up
of mercenaries who cared nothing about the empire. The lack
of maneuverability of the Byzantine forces against the lightning
unencumbered agility of the Turks also contributed to the loss
of territory. But probably the main reason for the success of the
Turks was Byzantine apathy and social disaffection within the
empire. "While the waves of Turkish invasion were sweeping
over Syria and Asia Minor," notes one critic, "the Byzantine
empire showed no sign of arresting its progress."[16]

With the death of Basil II, his elderly brother Constantine
VIII ascended the throne and ruled for the next three years.
Unfortunately, Constantine was not at all like his brother Basil.
Anna wastes no words on him in the *Alexiad*. From other
sources we learn that Constantine was dominated by gluttony,
sexual passions, gambling, and a life of luxury. Constantine's one
object in life, wrote the contemporary historian Michael Psellos,
was to enjoy himself to the full and squander the treasury he had
inherited.[17]

During his three-year reign Byzantium was threatened in the
west by the Normans and the Patzinaks from the north. Saracen
pirates, Afrikans, and Sicilians gained great strength and dominated the Mediterranean, especially the coast of the Adriatic
Sea.[18] In April 1027, the Roman Emperor Conrad II descended
on Italy, subjugated Beneventum and Capua, and gave the
Normans the right to establish themselves in the country to combat the Greeks.[19] Chalandon states that the power of Byzantium
in Italy declined after the Byzantine governor Basil Bojannes was
recalled to Constantinople in 1027.[20]

Constantine VIII died on November 12, 1028, and Romanos
III Argyros (1028-34), a distinguished member of the civil
aristocracy, ascended the throne when he married Constantine's
second daughter Zoe. Romanos was already married, but the
Church sanctioned his marriage to Zoe when his wife was induced to enter a nunnery. Anna bypasses Romanos III completely. Perhaps she felt as other historians did about him; he
was inept, vain, and tried to model himself on famous figures of
the past whom he could never emulate. Romanos III Argyros
abolished the *allelengyon;* the peasants could not afford to pay
the tax, and the powerful were not willing to do so. The loss of
revenue from the small independent farmers weakened the central
government and played right into the hands of the foreign
invaders.

During the reign of Romanos III, the Byzantine Empire suffered
from Saracen invasions. The Seljuk Turks penetrated the Armeno-
Byzantine frontiers in 1029. In 1030 the emir of Aleppo defeated
Romanos III. There was a devastating raid on Bulgaria in 1032.
Byzantine prestige was restored somewhat when the redoubtable
George Maniaces captured Edessa the same year. In 1033 the
Patzinaks again crossed the Danube and ravaged the Balkans.
The imperial palace reflected the climate of corruption existing

in the state. Romanos III, who despised Empress Zoe, kept her short of money and lived openly with a mistress. Zoe took young Michael the Paphlagonian as her lover. From what Psellos writes, Romanos III was deliberately drowned by Michael's friends on April 1034. On the same day Zoe married her young lover, who immediately ascended the throne as Michael IV (1034-41). Anna Comnena says nothing about his reign.

Michael IV was a capable ruler and a courageous general, but he was afflicted with epileptic fits which grew worse after he ascended the throne. Conditions forced him to debase the coinage; however, with the help of his brother, the eunuch, John Orphanotrophos, he succeeded in holding in check the military magnates of the provinces. During his seven-year reign there were four Patzinak invasions. The position of the Byzantine Empire in southern Italy was strengthened somewhat when George Maniaces seized the eastern part of Sicily, including Messina and Syracuse. In 1040 the Byzantines won back Bari. But while the Greeks made these territorial gains, several of the Byzantine provinces revolted. In 1040 western Bulgaria, Servia, and Zeta revolted and demanded their independence. That same year, Zoe was induced by John Orphanotrophos to adopt Michael Calaphates, the emperor's nephew, as her son. In 1043 a group of Turcomans forced the Byzantine frontier and captured the Byzantine governor Likhoudes.[21] The Normans captured Melfi, key city in Apulia, during the last year of the reign of Michael IV.[22] Byzantine control in the south of Italy had deteriorated.

Continual ill health forced Michael IV to retire to the monastery of Anargyri which he had built. He died on December 10, 1041, and on the same day, Zoe's adopted son ascended the Byzantine throne as Michael V Calaphates. Michael V's rule lasted only four months. The new emperor made the mistake of banishing Empress Zoe to Prinkipo. A popular uprising, joined by the civil party and the church, led to his overthrow. Michael V was deposed and blinded on April 20, 1042. There is no mention of him in the *Alexiad*. The two sisters Zoe and Theodora who, from all reports hated each other, ruled Byzantium jointly for the next three months.

Zoe and Theodora were extremely extravagant and squandered the imperial treasury. "In fact," observes Psellos, who served at the court as imperial treasurer, "all this squandering, together with the high standard of living, was the beginning of the utter decline in our national affairs and the cause of our subsequent humiliation."[23] The incompetence of the two sisters created the need for a new ruler. It was resolved when Zoe married her third husband, Constantine IX Monomachos on June 1, 1043, who ruled from 1042 to 1055. Constantine IX was a member of the antimilitary civil aristocracy.

Constantine IX did nothing to curb the extravagance of the sisters. Indeed, according to Psellos, he acquiesced in their luxurious habits. "Constantine's idea was to exhaust the treasury of its money," he writes, "so that not a single *obol* was to be left there."[24] Constantine instituted a capriciously extravagant building program which foolishly depleted the treasury. He tore down the Church of Saint George the Martyr (the Church of Saint George of Mangana), rebuilt it, altered the whole plan, rebuilt it again on a more artistic scale, altered the whole plan once more on a more lavish scale. "And the reason for it?" Psellos asks. Constantine wanted to rival other churches.[25] Anna refers to the monastery of Saint George known as Mangana, which Monomachos had built, but she makes no mention of the enormous sums that were spent to build it (III, 4, p. 80).

In 1045 Constantine IX reorganized the state-controlled University of Constantinople. This project to foster higher education was certainly commendable. What made it inappropriate at this time was that the money was badly needed for military and naval defenses to combat the foreign invaders who were attacking Byzantium on three frontiers. The School of Philosophy was under the able direction of the Neoplatonist Michael Psellos who was given the title of Hypatos (Chief or Consul of Philosophers). The School of Law, under the direction of the eminent jurist John Xiphilinos, who had the title of Nomophylax (Guardian of the Law), provided the state with civil servants. Many new posts were created at this time, which also increased the cost of the administration.

What especially lowered Byzantine morale was Constantine's wasting of the imperial treasures to satisfy the whims of his mistress Sclerina. Anna refers indirectly to the immorality of the reign of Monomachos to contrast the high morals of her grandmother Anna Dalassena. "The women's quarter of the palace had been thoroughly corrupt ever since Monomachos assumed the power of Emperor," she writes, "and had been disgraced by licentious 'amours' right up to my father's accession" (III, 8, p. 86).

To make certain of a more or less fixed revenue, Constantine IX debased the coinage, and farmed out the collection of taxes to tax-farmers. The tax-farmers collected a definite sum which they had to turn over to the state; however, they were free to manage the districts in any way they chose. Not only were the tax-farmers ruthless in the means they used to collect the taxes, but they overburdened the peasantry with taxes, only a small part of which they turned over to the state. Joan Hussey quotes Cecaumenos, who noted that in Georgia and in the theme of Mesopotamia, taxes were so oppressive that on one occasion whole families preferred to go over to the Muslims.[26]

Constantine also instituted the system of *pronoia,* which granted property to eminent Byzantines as a reward for certain services. These conditional grants in *pronoia* were a feudal device which strengthened the defenses of the Byzantine Empire and the military aristocracy; they also contributed to the progress of feudalization. Ostrogorsky explains that

the *pronoia* estate was not the private property of the pronoiar, but was inalienable . . . not heritable. Ownership and unlimited rights of disposition remained with the State, who granted it out and withheld it at discretion. But as long as it was in his possession the pronoiar was, however, the absolute lord and master of the estate granted him and of the peasants settled on it, and as a rule he would keep it until the end of his life.[27]

The peasants who settled on the estate became the *paroikoi* of the *pronoiar* and had to pay all their dues and taxes to him. The pronoia is the most marked characteristic of the form which Byzantine feudalism took.[28] The *pronoiars* and the tax-farmers were administrative entities in themselves, modeled after the state and existing side by side with it. The people had to pay the increasing burden. The *pronoia* was a sign of the weakness of the imperial government.[29]

During the reign of Monomachos, Byzantium was harassed by internal dissension as well as by foreign invasions. Civil wars squandered both resources and manpower. George Maniaces revolted in 1043 when Constantine IX arbitrarily deprived him of his post. Anna refers to "the famous George Maniaces who had mastered and subdued Sicily" (V, 8, p. 132). In 1048, the

Armenian Leo Tornicios rebelled and besieged Constantinople.
He capitulated and on December 24 was blinded. This was
another victory for the civil party. In 1043 the rest of Armenia was annexed, which removed yet
another buffer state and opened the way for the Seljuk Turks.
In 1046 Robert Guiscard arrived in Italy. The following year the
German emperor Henry III agreed to recognize the Norman
Rainulf as count of Aversa.[30] It was during the reign of Mono-
machos that Byzantine control in Italy deteriorated. The Normans
captured the theme of Longobardia, Byzantium's last possession
west of the Adriatic. Four Patzinak incursions devastated the
Balkan Peninsula during his reign. In 1048, Tirakh, khan of the
Patzinaks, launched a devastating invasion against the Byzantine
Empire, in reprisal against Kegan, another Patzinak chieftain
living securely within Greek territory who kept crossing the
Danube and attacking Tirakh. Monomachos might have avoided
this invasion had he heeded Tirakh's repeated protests.[31]

Empress Zoe died in 1050. The only mention of her name in
the *Alexiad* is associated with the gold and silver ornaments
which lay in her tomb, which her father had appropriated to
carry on the war against Robert and the Turks (VI, 3, p. 141).
In 1050-51 the Patzinaks continued their incursions. In 1053 the
Patzinaks defeated the Byzantine army in the Bulgarian city of
Preslav, near the Danube.[32] In 1054 the Seljuk sultan Tughril
Beg (1038-63) himself waged a holy war into Byzantine Armenia.

Constantine did nothing to stem the growing power of the
church over imperial authority. In 1054, Patriarch Michael Cerularios compelled Monomachos to accept the final schism between
the Latin and Orthodox churches. Anna makes no mention
whatever of the schism, although the tone of her writing certainly
reflects the anti-Latin climate which prevailed during her father's
reign. As Diehl observed, the final separation of the Eastern and
Western Churches in 1054, hastened the fall of Greek domination
in Italy and left a Christianity divided and weakened by internal
dissension face to face with a united Islam. The Latins thought
of the Greeks as schismatics, the Byzantines hated Rome.[33]
Alexios would have to use the most sensitive kind of diplomacy
to neutralize some of the anti-Greek hostility of the crusaders.

Constantine IX died on January 11, 1055, and the aged Theodora, the last of the Macedonian dynasty, became sole ruler from
1055 to 1056. Shortly before her death on August 31, 1056,

Theodora was induced by the civil party to nominate the aged Michael Stratioticos, who ruled Byzantium for one year (1056-57). The forces of the Seljuk sultan Tughril Beg were active during the one-year reign of this ruler. In 1057, the Turks plundered in the mountains of Trebizond and Khanzit. Several months later Malatya (Melitene) was devastated.[34]

From what Psellos writes, Michael Stratioticos conferred honors which surpassed propriety and caused disaffection. He also poured a "torrent of abuse" on Isaac Comnenos, chief man in a delegation of soldiers who went to interview him. The army rebelled and unanimously decided to place Isaac Comnenos on the throne.[35] The troops of the Armenian provinces were withdrawn to support Isaac Comnenos in his rebellion, which gave Samuk (Samoukht), the Turkish commander in Anatolia, the opening he needed to invade the regions where the two branches of the Euphrates join.[36]

Anna tells us a little more about the reign of her great uncle Isaac Comnenos, although she omits several important events in Isaac's struggle with the Seljuks. As our historian recalls the events of his reign, the Dacians had treacherously broken their treaty with the Romans, and the Sauromatae (Mysians) took advantage of the violation by migrating into Byzantine territory and mercilessly plundering the neighboring towns and districts. Emperor Isaac went to Triaditza, where he succeeded in checking the Dacians from further attacks on Roman territory (III, 8, 2, pp. 87-88).

Anna forgets to tell us of the sharp struggle her great uncle fought against Patriarch Michael Cerularios, who had united with the civil aristocracy for supremacy of the church over the emperor. During his short reign the Patzinaks joined the Hungarians in an attack on Byzantium. Isaac Comnenos went after them, settled peace with the Hungarians, then went after the Patzinaks who sued for peace even before any encounter took place. Isaac pursued one Patzinak chief named Selte who continued to ravage Greek territory, defeated him and destroyed his stronghold.[37] Although Isaac was unable to stop the Seljuk incursions he did go after a Turkish band which ravaged the Armenian provinces and had penetrated into Asia Minor.

Isaac abdicated in 1059 and designated as his successor Constantine X Ducas who ruled from 1059 to 1067. Ducas, a distinguished member of the civil aristocracy, an intimate friend

of Psellos and the Patriarch Constantine Leichudes, was married
to Eudocia Macrembolitissa, a niece of Michael Cerularios. It
was the civil party which made it possible for the antimilitary
Ducas to ascend the throne. Anna's reference to Constantine X Ducas reveals only his
relationship to the Ducas family (III, 3, p. 77). Perhaps Anna's
quick dismissal of the reign of this ruler was sparked by the
fact that Constantine X Ducas succeeded her great uncle when
her grandfather John Comnenos refused the crown.[38]

All historians agree that Constantine Ducas's antimilitary policy,
which satisfied the civil party, so diminished the military strength
of Byzantium that it opened the way for the invasions of Patzinaks, Uzes, and Seljuk Turks. Sir Charles Oman states that Constantine X "disbanded no inconsiderable portion of the army
and cut down the pay of the rest" in order to save money.[39]
Even the antimilitary Psellos criticizes Constantine for his treatment of foreign enemies:

international differences, according to his idea, had to be settled,
not by recourse to arms, but by the sending of gifts and by other
tokens of friendship—for two reasons: in the first place, he would
avoid having to spend the greater part of the imperial revenues on
the army, and secondly his manner of life would not be disturbed.
Actually he was greatly mistaken in this, for when the military
organization broke down, the power of our enemies increased and
they became more active in opposition.[40]

Eugen Stanescu asserts that in his political policy Constantine
followed a middle road, established new taxes, and aggravated
fiscal abuses. The practice of the collection of revenue reinforced
the corruption of the administration in general. Insufficient military machinery was the natural result of the general character
of these counterreforms.[41] Constantine Ducas farmed out taxes,
introduced the sale of offices, and neglected the army.

In 1059 Samuk succeeded in attacking Sebastea (Sivas). The
same year Robert Guiscard was recognized by Pope Nicholas II
as duke of Apulia, Calabria, and Sicily at the Council of Malfi.
Robert had already styled himself "by the grace of God and
St. Peter Duke of Apulia and Calabria and, with their help,
hereafter of Sicily."[42] In 1060, Robert had captured Reggio, Brin-
disi, and Taranto.[43] In 1061 his personal leadership enabled the
Normans to capture Messina. Tughril Beg died in 1063 and was

succeeded by his nephew Alp Arslan (1063-72), who immediately
undertook a massive assault on Armenia and on central Asia
Minor. Independent Turkish bands also raided Greek territories.
In 1064 the Hungarians occupied Belgrade. On July 6, 1064,
Alp Arslan annexed Ani, former capital of the Armenian kingdom,
and subjugated Armenia and Georgia. In the west the Patzinaks
joined by the Uzes ravaged Thrace and Macedonia. Constantine
marched against them with 150,000 men but before he could
join battle they had retreated over the Danube.[44] In 1067-68
they laid waste Cilicia, the country around Antioch, Armorium,
in Anatolia. In the same year Caesarea (Kayseri) in Cappadocia
was devastated.[45] Samuk continued his raids as far as Galatia
and Phrygia.[46]

From Speros Vryonis we learn another side of this Cappadocian
noble. In order to secure the support of the church and the
populace of Constantinople, Constantine admitted a great host
of artisans, craftsmen, and laborers into the Senate.[47] Psellos,
who admired Constantine X, states that during his reign,

not a single man of that assembly was sent away without some
reward. The government officials, their deputies, the minor dignitaries,
even the manual workers, all received something. In the case of
the last-named, he actually raised their social status. Until this time
there had been a sharp distinction between the class of ordinary
citizens and the Senate, but Constantine did away with it. Hence-
forth no discrimination was made between workers and Senators,
and they were merged into one body.[48]

Furthermore, he never inflicted corporal punishment on anyone,
no matter how dreadful the crime committed.[49]

After her husband's death on May 21, 1067, Eudocia Macrembolitissa, Constantine's second wife, acted as regent for her young
sons Michael VII, Andronicos, and Constantine, until her marriage to her second husband, General Romanos Diogenes, on
January 1, 1068. Romanos IV was a Cappadocian magnate, an
experienced and brave commander who had distinguished himself in the wars against the Patzinaks.

Anna covers the events in the reign of Romanos IV Diogenes
(1068-71) more fully, not only because her husband's history
covers this period, but because two of her uncles started their
military careers during his reign. Romanos had appointed Manuel,
older brother of Alexios, general in sole command over the whole

of Asia, while her uncle Isaac had been elected by lot as duke
of the principality of Antioch. She is prompted by filial devotion
to tell us that at the accession of Diogenes, her father had just
entered his brilliant youth (Preface, 3, p. 3). Anna gives credit
to Diogenes for having erected some fine houses in a place called
Aretae, which the Comneni had seized, and which was suitable
for kings for short periods of rest (II, 8, p. 62). She refers
sympathetically to Diogenes's two sons, Nicephoros and Leo,
both of them Porphyrogeneti (VII, 2, p. 170), to highlight the
fact that Alexios had taken them over "as private persons" upon
the death of their father (IX, 6, p. 224). She also proudly recalls
that Romanos IV admired her grandfather-in-law, Nicephoros
Bryennios, for his truthfulness in word and deed, and wanted to
adopt him as a brother (X, 3, p, 241). Significant to Anna is the
fact that Diogenes had issued coins of "ancient quality" with
his effigy on them (III, 10, p. 92).

Actually, Anna felt contempt for Romanos IV Diogenes because the barbarians first overran the boundaries of the Roman
Empire during his reign and kept advancing right down to her
father's reign. "Cities were wiped out, countries were laid waste,"
she writes, "and the whole Roman territory was defiled with the
blood of Christians" (XV, 10, 2, pp. 418-19).

Historians generally agree that Romanos was rash as a soldier.
However, Anna's appraisal of this unfortunate ruler whose life
ended so tragically, seems circumspectly limited. She admits
that Emperor Diogenes was on an "extremely arduous campaign
he was conducting against the Turks," but this concession is to
highlight the fact that her danger-loving father, who was fourteen
years old at that time, was anxious to join him in that campaign
(I, 1, p. 7).

Other sources inform us that Romanos made an effort to win
the friendship of the Normans by proposing the marriage of one
of his sons to one of Robert Guiscard's daughters. Guiscard
rejected this proposal.[50] Romanos went after the Seljuks a few
months after he ascended the throne, unfortunately with a poorly
organized army of foreign mercenaries. In 1068, he succeeded
in capturing Artah near Antioch and Manbij northeast of Aleppo.
The following year Diogenes went after the Turks in the region
around Caesarea in Cappadocia. Diogenes and Alp Arslan came
to an agreement, hopefully to stop both the Turkish raids and
Byzantine defensive attacks; then the sultan left on an expedition,

secure in the thought that the agreement would hold. Unfortunately, Turkish bands continued to raid Greek territory, either without the knowledge of Alp Arslan or in defiance of him. Under these circumstances the truce lost its validity, and Diogenes went after the Turks. When Alp Arslan learned that Diogenes was attacking the frontiers of his own states by way of Armenia, he hastily marched against him. On August 26, 1071, Alp Arslan captured Romanos at Manzikert near Lake Van. Alp Arslan released him when Romanos agreed to pay a ransom, promise an alliance, and restore the frontier strongholds that the Greeks had captured from the Turks in the preceding half century.[51] Diogenes was then given a Turkish guard and was allowed to return to his country. In the meantime, however, Romanos IV had been deposed by the civil party. On October 24, 1071, Michael VII was proclaimed sole emperor and his mother Empress Eudocia was immured in a nunnery.

As fate would have it, in April of the same year, Guiscard had captured the Adriatic seaport of Bari and conquered the other maritime towns of Apulia. In July 1071, Robert and his brother Roger entered the port of Catania as allies, treacherously conquered the town, and then laid siege to Palermo. On January 10, 1072, Palermo surrendered. After the fall of Palermo, Robert and Roger partitioned the island between themselves.[52] Robert turned his eyes to the Byzantine Empire.

Anna finds it unnecessary to discuss Romanos's disastrous defeat by the Turks at Manzikert because, she explains, his tragic end "had been treated by several historians" (IX, 6, p. 224). Anna avoids mentioning that if her maternal grandfather, Andronicos Ducas, who was in charge of the rear of the army, had not run away and deliberately spread the rumor that the battle was lost, Romanos might not have been defeated. Anna refers only indirectly to Diogenes's loss of sight without telling us anything of the intrigues of Emperor Michael Ducas who gave the order to blind Diogenes.

According to one Greek historian, three metropolitan bishops swore on the Bible to Romanos that if he returned to the capital nothing would happen to him. On the road, however, he was seized by the men of Michael Ducas; they tortured him, blinded him, then exiled him to the island of Propontis, where he died.[53] The only time Anna refers to Manzikert, again avoiding any mention of the name of the battle, is when her father asked

Kilij Arslan (1092-1107), son of Sulayman and theoretical ruler of Asia after the death of Malik Shah, to submit to the Roman Empire and live at peace in the countries assigned to him, "before Romanos Diogenes took over the reins of government and suffered that terrible defeat when he unfortunately joined battle with the Sultan and was captured by him" (XV, 6, p. 405). Romanos IV ruled three years and eight months to September 1071. He died in the summer of 1072.

Byzantine historians are agreed that the defeat of Manzikert was the most disastrous of all the wars against the Turks. Indeed, it was the beginning of the end for Byzantium. The Turcomans were now able to enter Rum without difficulty; it opened Asia Minor to Turkish conquest. I am inclined to agree with Hussey, who believes that it was the deposition of Romanos by the civil party, not his defeat at Manzikert, which brought on the civil wars and the conquest of Asia Minor by the Seljuk Turks which resulted in the Sultanate of Rum.[54] Proof of this is Anna herself, who writes that Philaretos, the Armenian general whom Romanos had raised to the rank of domestic, defected to the Turks because of the blinding of Romanos. "It was more than he could bear," Anna writes, "for he loved him with an exceeding love, so plotted rebellion and made himself master of the province of Antioch" (VI, 9, p. 153). The establishment of the Sultanate of Rum dates from the defection of Philaretos.

Michael VII, Anna's maternal great-grandfather, ruled from 1071 to 1078. Anna establishes Michael VII's relationship to Queen Maria and Maria's brother-in-law, Nicephoros Diogenes. She mentions him again in the official treaty between Alexios and Bohemond with regard to two hundred pounds of gold with the effigy of Michael VII. The Norman preferred the effigy on the coin of the man who had betrothed his son to Bohemond's sister (XIII, 12, p. 356).

Anna writes that during the reign of Michael VII, "the hegemony of the Romans had received several checks, and the luck of the Turks was in the ascendency and the Romans had been driven back like dust shaken from their feet ... The barbarian Tutach had just come down with a considerable army from the depths of the East to ravage Roman territory" (I, 2, pp. 7-8). Anna does not relate these Turkish advances to the treaty that Alp Arslan had made with Emperor Romanos, which was no longer in effect after Diogenes was blinded and Michael VII ascended the throne.

The Turks made this an excuse for the invasion and conquest of Byzantium. In 1072, Patzinaks and Uzes invaded the Empire. Alp Arslan died in January 1073 and his son Malik Shah (1072-92) became his successor. Malik Shah now progressed in Mesopotamia and Syria, gave Syria to his brother Tutush, and entrusted Sulayman as the founder of the Sultanate of Rum. We know from Anna that the Norman mercenary Ursel (Russel of Bailleul) proclaimed his independence in Asia Minor in 1073, because her father captured him and turned him over to the Emperor (I, 1,2,3, pp. 7-12). In 1073 the Patzinaks and Uzes invaded the Empire again. In 1074 Michael VII was forced to recognize the rule of Sulayman in order to obtain the support of Turkish mercenaries to suppress the revolt of John Ducas.[55] In 1075, Croatia gained its independence; two years later Zeta also gained its independence.

What Anna holds most against Michael VII is the betrothal of his son Constantine to Guiscard's daughter (later named Ilelen) which brought about the Norman invasion of the Empire (I, 15, p. 38). In 1079, Botaneiates dethroned Michael VII and the contract of this betrothal was no longer valid; Guiscard used this as an excuse to wage war against the Byzantine Empire. From another source we are informed that Michael wrote two letters to Robert Guiscard in 1071 or 1072, the other in 1072 or 1073, in which he asks for Guiscard's friendship by proposing marriage of the emperor's brother Constantine to one of Guiscard's daughters. Guiscard rejected both proposals. In 1074, Michael VII proposed marriage again, this time, however, of his own son Constantine with one of Guiscard's daughters. Guiscard accepted this proposal, and Michael VII issued a Chrysobull to Guiscard which bears the date August 1074[56] and confirms the conditions of their alliance. Michael hoped that with the assistance of the Normans he might be able to drive the Turks out of Asia Minor.[57]

Anna writes little else about Michael VII, who was Psellos's pupil, and whom he lauded as the "prodigy of our generation." Scylitzes blames Psellos for training Michael Ducas as he did: "while he spent his time in the useless pursuit of eloquence and wasted his energy on the composition of iambic and anapestic verse (and they were poor efforts indeed), he brought his empire to ruin led astray by his mentor the philosopher Psellos.[58] Scylitzes also criticizes Michael VII for having appointed the eunuch

Nicephoritza as *logothete*,[59] about whom he writes, "while he
(Nicephoritza, the emperor's favorite) concentrated all power
in his hands, Michael found time for nothing but trifles and
childish games. The leading philosopher Psellos had made him
quite unfitted for the position he occupied."[60] Anna also omits
telling us that Michael VII had written to Pope Gregory VII
begging him for help against the Turks and promising the re-
union of the churches. "The military aid requested for this
offensive was no doubt made a prerequisite for the union of the
churches," observes Charanis; when this was not forthcoming
Gregory VII must have learned "that the Greeks were no longer
anxious to bring about a unity of the churches." According to
this historian, it was for this reason that Gregory VII sanctioned
the Norman invasion.[61]

Anna concludes her remarks about Michael VII by telling us
that he was deposed by Nicephoros Botaneiates, embraced the
monastic life and was later invested with the alb and miter, and
the superhumeral of the archbishop (I, 12, p. 31). From her
husband we learn more specifically that Michael was ordained
and soon after was consecrated metropolitan of Ephesus by the
hand of Patriarch Thomas.[62]

Anna has contempt for the "old man" Nicephoros III Botaneiates who overthrew Michael VII with the assistance of the Seljuk
Turks and ascended the throne on March 24, 1078, at the age
of sixty. Understandably, Anna was against the ruler who was
so slavishly influenced by his Scythian favorites, Borilos and
Germanos, who almost succeeded in blinding her uncle Isaac
and her father. Anna was not exaggerating when she wrote that
Byzantium had sunk to its lowest ebb. It was true that the armies
of the east were dispersed in all directions. As she states, "the
Turks had overspread, and gained command of, nearly all the
countries between the Euxine Sea and the Hellespont, and the
Aegean and Syrian Seas, and the various bays, especially those
which wash Pamphylia, Cilicia and empty themselves into the
Egyptian Sea" (I, 4, p. 13).

During the reign of this ruler, the Byzantines of Nicaea and
Nicomedia opened the gates to Alp Arslan. The people were
so overburdened with taxes that they did not feel hostile to the
conquests of the Turks.[63] "It is now clear," writes Claude Cahen,
"that it was the Byzantines themselves who encouraged the
Turks to advance further than they would have done at once

of their own accord, and provided their leaders with the basis of solid power by throwing open to them towns which would have held out within their walls, at least for a time. Thenceforward Nicaea was Sulayman's capital."[64]

During the struggle for possession of the throne, following the overthrow of Michael VII, Patzinaks and Uzes found it easy to ravage the empire. Anna has already told us of the two rebellions which her father was summoned to crush. We also know from her that Robert was warring against the empire during the reign of the ruler. It was during the reign of Botaneiates that Robert's son Bohemond had seized Hydruntum (Otranto), Canina, and Valona (I, 14, p. 37). Robert returned to seize the fortified town of Corfu and was on his way to besiege Dyrrachium[65] when he heard of the revolt of Alexios for the Byzantine throne (I, 16, p. 40). We also know from Anna that the Turks were grievously harassing the frontiers in the east (III, 8, 2, p. 89). She tells us that Sulayman had his "sultanicium" at Nicaea, and his raiders devastated the territory around Bithynia and Thynia ceaselessly and even got as far as the Bosporos (III, 11, p. 93). We are also told that the Roman Empire was left with a small and inadequate army except for a few "Immortals"[66] and a few soldiers from Coma and a Celtic regiment[67] that had shrunk to a small number of men (I, 4, p. 13). By about 1080, Sultan Malik Shah was already in control of the entire territory of Asia Minor from Cilicia to the Hellespont and had founded the Sultanate of Rum. The year Alexios became emperor the Turks ruled from the Euphrates to the Sea of Marmora where Nicaea became the first capital of the Seljuk Sultanate of Anatolia.[68] On July 25, 1080, Pope Gregory sanctioned Guiscard's expedition against the Byzantine Empire.[69] Just before Alexios ascended the throne Bohemond had landed in Epirus and Guiscard made ready to follow him with 30,000 men.[70]

Anna neglects to tell us about the civil wars which continued from 1078 to 1081, and fostered the spread of Patzinak and Turkish power; there were hostilities during the reign of Botaneiates between the Greeks and the Bulgarians. Anna fails to relate the revolt of the Comneni to the political discontent of the people which surely helped them to succeed in their revolt; one suspects that she did this to focus even more sharply her father's popularity with the army.

Anna gives Botaneiates some credit for permitting Constantine

Ducas, her first fiancé, who had doffed the red buskins of his
own accord, "to wear silk shoes of varied colors," although he
"grudged him the splendor of entirely red buskins" (III, 4, p. 79).
She condemns Botaneiates for bypassing Constantine Ducas for
Synadenos as his successor to the throne. "The old man failed to
see," she writes, "that he was arranging matters in a way which
was not only unjust but also disastrous, and was begetting trou-
bles for himself" (II, 2, p. 46).

She blames Botaneiates for depleting the treasury, but she
does not specify that the treasury was empty partly because the
money was spent "to win partisans to whom he made large gifts
in the early days of his reign."[71] She also forgets to mention
that a result of his wastefulness was the mutiny of the Varangian
guard because they were unpaid; the army also was dissatisfied
and protested against the two Scythian favorites, Borilos and
Germanos, set over it.[72] Botaneiates created an additional prob-
lem which Anna fails to report. In his efforts to gain the support
of the aristocracy, Botaneiates had increased the number of
senatorial dignities to a very large number of beneficiaries, and
gave complete fiscal amnesty to all who had been in arrears at
the beginning of his reign. This annulled the political efficiency
of the Senate.[73] Alexios would have to use all his ingenuity to
alter the senatorial system.

These then were the ills that Alexios inherited when he ascended the throne in 1081. He found a depleted treasury, a debased
coinage, a greatly impaired central government; the system of
military small holdings had collapsed; consequently, there was
loss of native manpower; a decline in trade and taxes seriously
curtailed military and naval defenses, and there was a ring of
foreign invaders. Patzinaks were in the Balkans, the greater part
of Asia Minor was in the hands of the Seljuk Turks, and the Normans had complete mastery over all territory in Italy that had
formerly belonged to the Byzantine Empire. When Alexios ascended the throne, the Turks were in possession of Caesarea in
Cappadocia, Iconium, Philadelphia, Smyrna, Sebastea, Neo-
Caesarea.[74] Alexios was not overstating his need when he appealed to the Senate to allow him to appropriate unused church
vessels to carry on the war against Robert and the Turks. Anna, in
justification, has him say, "I found the Empire surrounded on all
sides by barbarians and absolutely deficient in resources . . . you
are not ignorant of the incursions of the Persians (the Turks) nor

of the raids of the Scythians, and you have not forgotten the spears of Lombardy that were whetted against us" (VI, 3, pp. 141-42).

Although Anna has omitted many of the specific causes of the decline of Byzantium from 1025 to 1081, she does give the reader an objective report of the difficulties confronting Alexios when he ascended the throne, difficulties which would have been insurmountable for a less talented ruler. It is true that Anna's account of these years is telescoped in the *Alexiad*; however, we do have some understanding of the reasons for the extreme measures the young emperor had to take to overcome these difficulties. Awareness of these ills will help us to evaluate the achievements of her father as Anna unfolds them for us in the *Alexiad*.

CHAPTER 2

Anna, Byzantine Princess

I Origin and Rise of the Comneni

The Comneni came originally from Comne, near Hadrianople, and
had estates in the Castamon district of Asia Minor. (Michael Psellos,
Fourteen Byzantine Rulers, the Chronographia, translated by E. R. A.
Sewter, p. 276, n. 3)

FROM the very first page of the *Alexiad* the reader is immediately struck by Anna's pride in her own royal birth as a
Comnena and the origin of her relatives and other personages
close to her father. To be sure, birth was not as important as
achievement in Byzantine Greece, nor was it to Anna; nonetheless,
our Byzantine historian never misses an opportunity to mention
the aristocratic origin of her subjects in all the dramatic pen
portraits amply strewn in the *Alexiad.* Byzantine scholars have
found it strange, therefore, that neither Anna nor her husband,
whose unfinished history of the reign of Alexios she used as a
primary source for the *Alexiad,* have anything to say about the
origin of her father's military landowning family that ruled
Byzantium for one hundred and four years. This omission appears
all the more puzzling, since both Anna and her husband went
to such great lengths to trace the origins of the Ducas family.

G. Murnu[1] accepts without verification Karl Hopf's statement,
discovered in the travels of Benjamin of Tudela, who visited
Byzantium during the reign of Anna's nephew Manuel Comnenos
(1143-80). Tudela's statement declares that Manuel Comnenos
showed particular sympathy toward the Vlachs who were people
of the same race. Murnu explains that the Vlachs were proved
by N. Iorga and others to have had a "privileged situation under
the Comneni."

Georgina Buckler does not accept Murnu's statement, observing
that "the *Strategicon* of Cecaumenus has a most violent diatribe
against the Vlachs, as false, treacherous and cowardly." She notes
38

further that she does not put much stock in Anna's mention of the Vlachs in four of her father's campaigns; "nothing as to any 'privileged position' can be learned from Anna," she writes, "and to a 'Roman' princess any half-breed nomadic stock would hardly be an ancestry to be proud of."[2]

A careful reading of Anna's references to the Vlachs in the context in which they appear reveals nothing which can possibly be identified with the origin of her father's family. Anna's first mention of the word Vlach occurs in her account of a campaign against Bohemond. She tells us that her father marched to Ezeba (modern Nezeros), "a Vlach village situated close to Androneia" (V, 5, p. 126). In another account of a campaign against the Patzinaks, Anna writes that her father ordered his brother-in-law Nicephoros Melissenos "partly to levy recruits from the Bulgarian and from nomadic tribes (called Vlachs in popular parlance)" (VIII, 3, 2, p. 199). Recounting the events of a campaign against the Cumans, Anna mentions by name, "a certain Pudilus, a Vlach nobleman," who one night warned her father that the Cumans were crossing the Danube. This decided Alexios "to assemble the leading men among his relations and officers at dawn of day and consult on the steps to be taken" (X, 2, 5, p. 239). Anna adds that in the same campaign the Vlachs also showed the paths over the passes to her father's enemies the Cumans (X, 3, p. 240).

M. Gyoni believes that Anna referred to the imperial map for her *Alexiad;* she mentions the Bulgarians and the Vlachs because they were the two ethnic groups of Bulgaria from which Nicephoros Melissenos was instructed by Alexios to recruit men. Gyoni believes that people who drew up the imperial maps always preferred precise terms. Although Anna would certainly have preferred to use the Attic terms for the Vlachs, she was forced to use the popular name of the Bulgarians for the simple reason that her mother's family was of Bulgarian origin. When Anna read her father's map of 1091, she used the names noted on the map. M. Gyoni sees no relationship of the Vlachs to the origin of the Comneni.[3]

Chalandon is also puzzled by the fact that neither Nicephoros Bryennios nor his wife make any mention of the origin of the Comneni, especially since they write so freely on the origin of the Ducas family and their alliance with the house of the Bulgarian czars.[4] The testimony of Psellos stated above also makes no mention of Vlachs in this connection.

What can perhaps be drawn with some justification from the references given above is that the origin of the Comneni may not have been as noble as Byzantine scholars customarily have believed. Anna and her husband must have had personal reasons for omitting this information from their histories. Of course, Anna's haughty spirit would never allow her to dwell at length on any humble family beginnings; however, there is no conclusive proof that the Comneni were of Vlach origin. Whatever the reason may have been for Anna's omission of the origin of her father's family, the reader must keep in mind that Byzantium was, as L. Oeconomos correctly observes, "an immense mosaic of different nationalities united by their alliance of Christianity with Hellenism."[5] Their cultural and their national conscience was Hellenic; whatever their origin, they were Byzantines.

The name Comnenos first appeared in Byzantine history during the reign of Basil II (976-1025). Byzantine chroniclers mention Nicephoros, governor of Vaspurakan (district of Van), and Manuel, a servant and friend of Basil II, whom the emperor called Eroticos, although his family name was Comnenos.[6] We must turn to the *Hyle Historias* of Nicephoros Bryennios, if we wish to know more about the place and lineage of the Comneni. From her husband then, we learn that Anna's great-grandfather Manuel Comnenos "was designated plenipotentiary to reconcile by treaty Basil, Emperor of the Romans" and the insurrectionist Bardas Scleros whom he subdued, "thanks to his ability and his energy."[7] Anna repeats this story about her great-grandfather in connection with a tower in Nicaea which had acquired its name Gonatas during Manuel's defense of Nicaea (XI, 1, 2, pp. 270-71). From Bryennios we also learn that on his deathbed Manuel committed his two motherless sons, Isaac and John, to Basil's care. The emperor accepted his charges and sent them to Studium monastery where Isaac and John were placed in the care of pedagogues whose duty it was "to shape the character of young men" and to train them in virtue and in the art of military warfare.[8]

Like most sons of the nobility, after John and Isaac had completed their studies, they entered the regiment of the imperial guard where they held high office. Isaac married Catherine (or Aecaterina), eldest daughter of Samuel, former king of the Bulgarians; his brother John, Anna's paternal grandfather, married Anna Dalassena, daughter of Alexios Charon, on whom the emperor had conferred the command of Italy. Anna makes only three allusions to her great-uncle Emperor Isaac: once to identify a certain Docianos, nephew of Emperor Isaac and her father's cousin (I, 3, 2, p. 12); a second time, to explain how it happened that the chapel of the martyr Thecla, where her grandmother worshipped, had been built by her great-uncle Emperor Isaac (III, 8, 2, p. 87); and her third allusion simply states that her great-grandfather Manuel was the father of Emperor Isaac (XI, 1, 2, p. 271). From Michael Psellos we learn that Emperor Isaac had a son who died young and a daughter named Maria who became a nun sometime after 1057.[9]

Bryennios informs us that John Comnenos, Anna's paternal grandfather, had five sons: Manuel, Isaac, Alexios (subject of the *Alexiad*), Adrian, and Nicephoros, and three daughters: Maria, Eudocia, and Theodora, all of whom survived their father and were present at his death.[10] All three historians mentioned above refer to one Docianos, son of a sister of John Comnenos. Anna mentions this Docianos as her father's cousin who at first denounced Alexios for blinding the rebel Ursel; when he discovered that it was "Palamedian playacting," he embraced and kissed Alexios repeatedly (I, 3, 2, p. 12).

From another source we learn that Anna's great-uncle Isaac won renown as a valiant general in the war against the Turks.[11] With the aid of the army and the assistance of the church, headed by Patriarch Michael Cerularios, the aged king Michael VI Stratioticos abdicated, and Isaac Comnenos was crowned by the patriarch in Hagia Sophia on September 1, 1057.[12] Vryonis asserts that among those present at the coronation were the heads of all the guilds.[13] However, Isaac's accession was a victory for the Asian military party over the European army, the bureaucracy, and the Senate.[14]

For the support of the patriarch, which Isaac lived to regret, he renounced a certain degree of jurisdiction over church affairs, which to that time had come within the province of the emperor. Puffed by his power, the patriarch went so far as to wear the purple buskins, the prerogative of the emperor.[15] In November 1058, Isaac had the patriarch arrested; when he refused to abdicate, Psellos, at Isaac's request, drew up the *Accusation* charging the patriarch with treason and heresy, supporting soothsayers, and dabbling in magic. However, Cerularios died on his way to be tried and was succeeded by Patriarch Leichudes in February 1059.[16] After the death of Patriarch Cerularios, Isaac regretted his treatment of him and granted his family "the privilege of speaking freely in his presence, and they were allowed to join his nearest retinue."[17]

But it was not Cerularios alone who brought about Isaac's voluntary abdication two years after he began what was predicted to be a great future for his reign, anticipating a time of wonderful prosperity.[18] Isaac defended the eastern border against the attacks of the Seljuks and gave both the Patzinaks and the Turks strong opposition.[19] He maintained peace with Egypt and in 1059 led an expedition against the Hungarians and the Patzinaks.[20] Isaac alienated the church and began to lose the support of the nobility and the army when he initiated many reforms necessitated by the depleted treasury which the last five of his predecessors had exhausted "on personal whims."[21] He abolished many pensions conferred on senators, nobles, and courtiers, who had no duties to perform; he diminished the expenditures of the imperial household; he exacted the payment of taxes from the nobility with merciless rigor.[22] Psellos found Isaac's actions worthy. What he criticized was Isaac's desire to do everything at once; he went too far in his reforms; he chose the wrong time and showed lack of restraint. That is to say, Psellos criticized most the method Isaac used to initiate these changes.[23]

Joannes Scylitzes, a contemporary who held the office of *protovestarios*[24] and *curopalates*,[25] and is recognized for his history of the period from the accession of Isaac to Alexios I, approved of the conduct of Isaac in curtailing the income of the monks. "Isaac was a man of fixed habits," he wrote; "he was fair-minded, sharpwitted, strong, intelligent, a great leader in war, a terror to his foes, kindly to his friends."[26] George Finlay criticizes Isaac for arrogantly changing the type of the gold coinage of the empire (the *laburum*) and having impressed on it his own figure with a drawn sword in his right hand, thereby ascribing his elevation to the throne not to the grace of God but to his own courage.[27] Finlay ignores the fact that Isaac made a bold attempt to strengthen the neglected military defences of the empire. His figure on the gold coin, with a drawn sword in his right hand, was his way of impressing his policy on the antimilitary civil party.

Isaac, who was passionately devoted to crane hunting, caught a chill, after which he decided to abdicate. Both Anna and her husband state clearly that Emperor Isaac offered the crown to his brother John, on whom he had conferred the dignity of *curopalates,* and that John refused it. In his *Hyle* Bryennios records the words that Isaac told his brother when he offered him the crown:

Oh my very dear brother, the end of my life is approaching and I am in immediate danger of dying. It is necessary that you make secure the direction of affairs and that you accept the help of the Empire. This decision will be profitable to our family, but still more to all our subjects of the Roman Empire. Then let yourself put on the diadem while I still breathe and consent to rule. Indeed, you know of the ambition of many men who are lying in wait for our power.[28]

Psellos's report of this incident differs radically from that of Anna or her husband. This contemporary historian makes no mention whatever of Isaac's brother; he writes that Isaac offered the crown directly to Constantine X Ducas. In his *Chronographia,* Psellos also reports what Isaac told Constantine when he offered him the crown: "Of those who stand around me here," Isaac said, "one is my brother, another my nephew, and, dearest of all, here is my wife, the empress, and here my daughter, my only child, in fact. But my choice falls on you rather than on them. Your qualities have a greater claim on me than the ties of kinship. It is to you I bequeath the Empire."[29] As has already been stated, Psellos was a member of the civil party. The church and the civil aristocracy were responsible for the overthrow of Isaac Comnenos.[30] Chalandon notes that it was only when Psellos had acclaimed Constantine that Isaac decided to retire to the Studium monastery where he had once received his education and where he died two years later.[31]

After Isaac's death, his wife Catherine changed her name to Helene and retired to a convent with her daughter Maria. She celebrated the anniversary of her husband's death by an annual religious memorial service during which she made a liberal distribution of alms. Her last command was to have her body interred in the cemetery of Studium as a simple nun, with no sign to indicate that she had been a Bulgarian princess and a Roman empress.[32]

John Comnenos died six years after Isaac, but he lived to see two of his daughters married to wealthy men of high birth: his

eldest daughter Maria married Michael Taronites, later honored
by Alexios with the title of Panhypersebastos; his younger daughter Eudocia married Nicephoros Melissenos, originating from
the family of Bourtzos, who, according to Bryennios, was "a man
full of sense and worthy of admiration."[33]

Thus it was that the Comneni rose to the power of the throne.
Twenty-two years would pass before another Comnenos would
become emperor of Byzantium.

II   *Anna Dalassena, Mother of the Comneni*

whatever decrees she gives in writing . . . shall have abiding validity
just as if they had been dispensed by my own serene Majesty or
ordered by my own word of mouth. (*Alexiad*, III, 6, 3, pp. 83-84)

The lines quoted above are taken from the chrysobull which
Alexios wrote five months after he ascended the throne as he
was preparing to go after Robert Guiscard who had crossed over
to Epirus. The chrysobull is recorded in the *Alexiad* in its
entirety, just as Alexios had written it, Anna avows, omitting only
the scribe's embellishments (III, 6, 2, pp. 83-84).

In this imperial document, published for the whole world to
see, Alexios granted his mother absolute power to rule in his
absence whenever he was forced to be away from Constantinople
on military matters. For the very significant role that Anna
Dalassena played in the lives of her sons, history has conferred
upon her the title of Mother of the Comneni.

Anna eulogizes her grandmother in two chapters of Book
III, though she admits that she knew her only slightly. It is interesting to note that Bryennios is even more lavish in his praise of
his wife's grandmother. Perhaps subconsciously Anna did not
relish recalling the hatred of Anna Dalassena for her mother's
family, or that her father "hung on her counsels" even after his
marriage to her mother. It was no secret that until Anna
Dalassena's retirement at the convent of Pantepoptes in 1100,
Anna's mother took second place not only in the imperial court
but also in her personal life. It was Anna Dalassena who was the
power behind the throne; it was Anna Dalassena who was first
among the women in the imperial household, and very often first,
as Anna tells us, in the rule of the empire.

Whatever our historian's innermost feelings may have been,
as she writes of this indomitable woman after a lapse of forty

years, she is unstinting in praise for her awesome grandmother
who had once governed all their lives. No other account in the
Alexiad throws more light on the life led in the imperial court
during the reign of her father than Anna's pen portrait of her
grandmother. The picture we get of Anna Dalassena is of an
imposing, ambitious, dominating, and humorless but politic
matriarch, spending her afternoons worshiping at the chapel of
Saint Thecla, chanting psalms and offering prayers in the
evening, a martinet when it came to the slightest deviation from
orthodoxy and piety. She was in complete command of the
unusual role she was destined to play in the imperial, military,
and social lives of her children and even of her grandchildren.

Anna Dalassena was the daughter of a high imperial func-
tionary of Italy, a nobleman of a powerful Asiatic family who
had earned the nickname Charon because each time he struck an
enemy he killed him. On her mother's side she was a descendant
of the illustrious Adrian and Theophylactos Dalassenos, whose
renown challenged several emperors. Anna traces her grandmother's descent from the Dalassenian Hadrians and Charons
(III, 8, 1, p. 86). According to Peter Charanis, the family originally came from Dalassa, a place which Adontz claims was an
Armenian center; on this ground, he writes, it may be that Anna
Dalassena was of Armenian origin.[34]

Anna Dalassena had been sharpened on the razor's edge of
court intrigue, but it was her own natural gifts that had
equipped her for her marriage to John Comnenos. "She had a
wonderful mind, truly loyal and worthy of the throne," writes
her granddaughter. "It was quite wonderful how she seemed to
have an old head on young shoulders" (III, 6, p. 82; 7, p. 85).
Anna showers encomiums on her grandmother for her majestic
dignity, her piety, and her high virtue, "which restored a commendable state of morals in the palace." She praises her grandmother's compassion for the poor, her kindness to priests and
monks, her intellect (III, 8, 1, p. 86).

While the *Alexiad* offers the reader no definite information on
the type of education of the Comneni children, Anna does
inform us that her father had received a good education from
infancy (III, 5, p. 80). We know that in Byzantium all sons of
the nobility were trained in philosophy, grammar, the Bible,
and in particular the classics, especially Homer, whose works
had to be memorized.[35] From Theophylactos, who taught

Constantine Ducas, Anna's first fiancé, we learn that the boy
was given physical exercises, horsemanship, the chase, and
management of the lance, and the bow and arrow. These were
mingled with the teaching of history and intellectual exercises
to ennoble language and to develop the mind. Referring to this
source, Chalandon concludes that the same education must have
been given to Alexios.[36]

In the early part of her history Anna tells us that in his childhood her father was imbued with such a fear of God that when
his soldiers plundered and pillaged Constantinople the day he
was proclaimed emperor, he was filled with terror of "the
divine anger lest he be altogether accursed of God" (III, 5, p.
80). In his chrysobull Alexios credits his mother for his successful ascension to the throne. "It was her prayers of great
frequency throughout her life," he writes, "that have reached the
ears of the Lord and have raised me to my present position of
sovereign" (III, 6, 3, p. 83). When Alexios investigated the
Manichaean heresy, Anna explains that her father, whom she
calls "the thirteenth apostle," "had studied the Holy Writings
more than anyone else in order to sharpen his tongue for
wrestlings with the heretics" (XIV, 8, 5, p. 386). From Nicephoros
Bryennios we learn that Anna Dalassena had provided her two
youngest sons, Adrian and Nicephoros, still children at the time
of her husband's death, with "tutors charged to give them well-
rounded instruction."[37]

Anna Dalassena's one bitterness was that her husband did not
succeed his brother when Isaac abdicated in 1059. Since she
could do nothing to change matters, she concentrated on her
children's careers, planning these with keen strategy. When her
husband died in 1067, three of their sons were already young
men of nineteen or twenty; two daughters had married while
their father lived, no doubt to men their mother had selected
for them. As has already been stated, Maria had married Michael
Taronites; the second daughter Eudocia married Nicephoros
Melissenos.

Soon after the death of her husband, Anna Dalassena attached
herself to her relative, Queen Macrembolitissa and Emperor
Romanos IV Diogenes (1067-71). It was the Mother of the
Comneni who was probably responsible for the mates of all her
children and her grandchildren. Although Queen Maria Alania
wanted Isaac, Anna Dalassena arranged for Isaac to marry Irene,

daughter of the prince of the Alains and cousin of the empress of Alania. There is no mention anywhere of any opposition when Alexios married his first wife Irene, daughter of Argyros, "a rich noble and proprietor of immense domains." When after her death Alexios sought to marry Irene Ducas, his mother intrigued mercilessly to prevent the marriage. However, this was one time when she could not cope with the forces against her; despite her intrigues the marriage took place in January 1078. Bryennios informs us that Anna Dalassena arranged for her youngest daughter Theodora to marry Constantine, son of Emperor Diogenes, when his father was on the throne. He admits that Constantine was noble and valiant, but his character was not praiseworthy on all points.[38] This marriage, which ended unhappily, was probably arranged for political reasons by Anna Dalassena, since she was attached to Romanos Diogenes.[39] We know from Anna that Theodora was married to Leo, another son of Romanos Diogenes, no doubt also arranged by Anna Dalassena (X, 2, 3, p. 238).

But above all else, the Mother of the Comneni kept her eye on the throne. In keeping with the preferred social position of the military man in the feudal aristocracy of Byzantium, she saw to it that all her sons entered a military career favoring the ruling party and that she herself was held in favor at the court. From Bryennios we learn that her firstborn son Manuel had entered a military career while his father was alive.[40] Romanos Diogenes had appointed him *protostrator;*[41] soon after he was elevated to supreme commander of all the troops of the East as a reward for his successes in the war against the Turks. Later, however, he was captured by the Turks, along with Melissenos and Taronites, but Manuel cleverly maneuvered their way to freedom by convincing the Turkish Chrysoskoulos, who rivaled the Sultan, to ally himself with the Romans, and thus, the three returned safely. In the spring, however, when Manuel started with Chrysoskoulos against the Turks in Bithynia, he was seized with an earache which led to his death.

When Anna Dalassena, who was in Constantinople, learned of Manuel's illness, which had taken a turn for the worse, that intrepid woman traveled to Bithynia, crossed Mount Azalas with the natives, and found her son at the point of death in a monastery. Manuel died in his mother's arms. Anna Dalassena stayed long enough to render her son the funeral honors he deserved.[42] It is difficult to understand why Anna states that her grandmother "did not know where she had buried the elder of her sons" (I, 1, p. 7).

Anna writes of her uncle Manuel, whose untimely death crushed his mother, as "a man who had done great and admirable deeds for his country" (I, 1, p. 7). She repeats her husband's account of Manuel's military career and mentions his name once again in connection with the revolt of the Comneni.

Alexios was fourteen years of age when his brother Manuel died. As Anna informs the reader, it was then that her father sought to join Emperor Diogenes on the campaign he was conducting against the Turks. This places the birth of Alexios in 1056. However, on that occasion Emperor Diogenes did not allow Alexios to accompany him, because Anna Dalassena was mourning the death of Manuel. "In order that she might not be inconsolable," writes Anna, "he compelled the boy Alexios to return to his mother" (I, 1, p. 7).

Probably the greatest role of Anna Dalassena, for which she was eminently suited, was the political role she played in the destiny of Alexios. When Emperor Romanos was defeated by the Turks in Manzikert, in 1071, Anna Dalassena, who was *curopalatissa*, remained faithful to the throne. The new ruler accused her of being in secret correspondence with Romanos and she was summoned before a tribunal. When confronted with the accusation, she produced a crucifix and brandished it in the faces of the judges, saying, "Here is my judge and yours. Think of Him when you sentence me and see that your sentence is worthy of the Supreme Judge who knoweth the secrets of the heart."[43] Anna Dalassena was banished with her sons to one of the prince's islands. There, as she probably anticipated, she was recalled from banishment when the Caesar John Ducas soon fell out with his nephew, Emperor Michael VII, and he was obliged to leave the court.

It was obvious from the role that the Mother of the Comneni played before and during the actual revolt of the Comneni that without her help Alexios might never have ascended the throne. From her granddaughter's report, it was on the advice of their mother that Alexios and her uncle Isaac planned their revolt. It was on her advice that Isaac, related by marriage to Empress Maria of Alania, encouraged her to adopt his brother Alexios, thus making him also a member of the imperial family and giving him full access to the palace. Anna devotes three pages to her grandmother's careful plans for the escape of her two sons on the night when they prepared to ride away from Constantinople. The Comneni had locked the gates and given their mother the keys. With magnificent control and mastery over the situation, she assembled all the women of the imperial household and led them, along with her two sons, to the Forum of Constantine, presumably to worship in the Church of God. This gave the Comneni time to arm themselves and make their escape safely out of the capital. Anna Dalassena then cleverly took refuge in the Sanctuary, a church where people accused of crimes found protection. When the emperor's messengers came to lead her back to the palace, as her granddaughter tells us, she clung to the "royal doors" of the Sanctuary, collapsed, and cried out, "Unless my hands are cut off, I shall not leave these holy precincts until I receive the Emperor's cross as a pledge of my safety" (II, 5, p. 54). The emperor did as she asked and gave her full immunity, confining all the women in the convent of Petrii with orders that their private possessions be preserved intact. The sympathetic guards and soldiers kept her informed about the progress her sons were making (II, 5, pp. 52-55).

On the day of her son's coronation, Anna Dalassena appeared in the monastic habit and carried no imperial insignia whatever.[44] After Alexios ascended the throne, Anna Dalassena instituted a strict regimen in the palace. Her granddaughter has left an account of her grandmother's daily routine:

for she had stated times for sacred hymns and fixed hours for breakfast and for attending to the election of magistrates, and she herself became a rule and measure for everybody else, and the palace had somewhat the appearance of a holy monastery. . . . But above all she honored priests and monks and nobody ever saw her at table without some monks. Her character as outwardly manifested was such as to be revered by the angels, and dreaded by the very demons. . . . Moreover, although she was very busy with public business, she never neglected the rules of conduct of the monastic life, but spent the greater part of the night in singing hymns, and became worn out with continual prayer and want of sleep; yet at dawn, and sometimes even at the second cock-crow, she would apply herself to State business, deciding about the election of magistrates and the requests to petitioners. (III, 8, pp. 86-87)

Anna Dalassena was behind every important move of her children. It was she who called the Patriarch Cosmas to help quiet Alexios's conscience about the sack of Constantinople when he and his troops pillaged their way into the capital after he was acclaimed emperor (III, 5, p. 80). To please his mother, Alexios even contemplated a divorce. It was the patriarch Cosmas, loyal to the house of Ducas, who prevented this. Anna recalls her grandmother's hostility to the Ducas family. "The family Ducas had long recognized the undisguised hatred the Mother of the Comneni bore them," she writes; "they lived in constant dread and suspicion of her as I have repeatedly heard them tell" (III, 2, p. 73). To prevent the coronation of Irene, Anna Dalassena demanded the resignation of Patriarch Cosmas. Her granddaughter writes with astuteness that "the holy man was not blind to these machinations" and swore that he would not resign until Irene received the crown from his hands (III, 2, p. 76). Anna Dalassena was obliged to accept the Patriarch's decision when she saw that the greater part of the nobility insisted on Irene's coronation. George Palaeologos, Irene's brother-in-law, stated publicly that he and his men had helped Alexios to the throne for Irene's sake. Irene was thus crowned seven days after that event. Cosmas resigned, and Anna Dalassena replaced him with the monk Eustratios Garidas.

After Alexios was securely enthroned, the Mother of the Comneni toyed for awhile with the idea of entering a monastery, because piety meant most to her. Alexios, however, dissuaded her, and she became reconciled to spending her life in the service of her son.

The chrysobull made Anna Dalassena more empress than Irene. For some twenty years Alexios permitted his mother to rule the empire jointly with him. Indeed, from what Anna writes, she was for a time the true chief of the empire, and the emperor seemed only the executor of her wishes (III, 6, 3, pp. 83-84.)

The two seals of Anna Dalassena that have been preserved reveal succinctly the true nature and position of this indomitable
                                                                    +
woman. One of them has on it: "Lord, Protect Anna Dalassena A, mother of the king." The letter A after her name has been taken by some scholars to mean *first;* however, the cross over the A is the classic abbreviation for nun.[45] In reality then, Anna Dalassena

signed, "nun, mother of the king." On the right side of the second
seal, we see the configuration of the Virgin of Blachernae; on the
other side, her full face with the medallion of the infant on her
breast, and the words: "Virgin, help thy servant Anna Dalassena,
nun and curopalatissa."[46] Although she thought of herself as
a "nun" there is no question that Anna Dalassena was the First
Lady of Byzantium during her lifetime.

Zonaras writes that Alexios grew to resent his mother's real
management of affairs, but he was in awe of her and allowed her
to go on ruling. Zonaras also writes that people attributed to her
all the evils of the empire.[47] Anna notes that it was her grandmother who gave the order to blind the pseudo-Diogenes, whom
they succeeded in capturing (X, 4, 1, p. 244-45).

Anna Dalassena did not wait to be thrust aside by her son.
Toward the year 1100 she retired voluntarily to the convent of
Pantepoptes, which she herself had founded. There she lived to a
ripe old age, venerated as the mother of the king and as the
true founder of the Comneni dynasty.[48] She died there about
1105,[49] on the very day it was predicted that she would die
(VI, 7, 1, p. 150).

The Mother of the Comneni played a significant role in her
son's reign. She was an indefatigable force in establishing the
Comneni dynasty. As a mother-in-law, however, indications are
that she was a domineering, meddlesome woman, who must
have made life quite difficult for Empress Irene. It was only after
Anna Dalassena's retirement that Irene had the opportunity not
only to act as regent but also to be a desired partner and wife
to Alexios.

III   *Alexios and Isaac*

It is said that the friends Orestes and Pylades had such a deep love
for each other that in time of battle either would be quite indifferent
to his own foes but would ward off those who attacked his friend,
and either would offer his own breast to receive the darts thrown at
the other. Exactly the same phenomenon could be witnessed in the
case of these two. (*Alexiad*, II, 1, p. 45)

No other member in her immediate family awakens Anna's love
as much as does her uncle Isaac, Alexios's older brother by a few
years. Not even her grandmother, whom she admired enormously,

gives Anna the pleasure she seems to feel when she is writing about her uncle Isaac.

From her description the two brothers looked very much alike; they were both dark eyed and had black, arched eyebrows. She tells us that her uncle Isaac "was like his brother in stature, and not very different from him in other respects, his complexion however was paler, and his beard less thick than his brother's especially around the jaws" (III, 3, p. 77). From the fuller description she gives of her father, it is safe to assume that they were not especially tall, but were well proportioned to their height and muscularly built. According to his daughter, Alexios did not cut an imposing figure when he stood; but when he was seated on the throne, he suffused awe and confidence. He said little; his eyes and the expression on his face spoke for him. When he did speak, however, "fiery eloquence dwelt on his lips" (III, 3, p. 76).

The lifelong friendship between Alexios and Isaac was deeply rooted in common interests shared from early childhood. As all boys of the nobility were wont to do, they too must have enjoyed hunting together, shooting arrows, hurling their spears and indulging in horse exercises. Anna tells us that "both the brothers often indulged in the chase if there was no great stress of business" (III, 3, pp. 77-78). They probably often played chess together, as Anna intimates when she writes that her father played chess with one of his relatives (XII, 6, p. 312). Both men were given an excellent education and both were passionately fond of theology and philosophy. In the trials of Italos, Nilos, and Basil the Bogomil, the brothers were an unbreakable team in their missionary zeal to stamp out the heresy that was mushrooming throughout the Byzantine Empire. They both enjoyed religious controversy, but, according to Anna, Isaac was more politic about arguing with heretics. Alexios relied heavily on his brother's assistance in matters of heresy.

But the chief pleasure which bound the two brothers "they found in military, rather than hunting adventures" (III, 3, p. 78). Both men were "lovers of danger." Both men were expert in warfare, not as armchair theoreticians, but as practical warriors who had been tested time and again by stern experience. Actually, Alexios began his military career as a lieutenant under his brother Isaac when he was commander of the East and West during the reign of Michael VII Ducas. Anna recognizes that when Michael

Ducas promoted Alexios to the rank of commander-in-chief of the Roman army, Isaac was as conspicuous a favorite as her father. Both men were invited together to share the emperor's tables and came to be identified as one. Bryennios writes of his wife's father:

No down flowered yet on his face; but already he showed his future strategic virtues and that long before maturity.... He collaborated with his brother, arranged the men in battle, commanded battalions and distinguished himself at the head of phalanxes in imaginary combats; in short, before being put to the proof, he showed himself expert in all military exercises.[50]

The brothers were also united by their reverence for their mother. Anna often focuses her historical lens on the esteem the brothers felt for Anna Dalassena. Our historian gives several instances which reveal the fraternal bond of love for their mother. At a critical point in the fortunes of Alexios, just before he took over the capital as the newly acclaimed emperor, the Comneni halted their advance, thus losing precious time, because they wondered if they should not first go to salute their mother and then proceed to the palace (II, 12, p. 68). Fortunately, the Caesar John Ducas prevented the delay by upbraiding them severely for their dilatoriness. Another time, when Isaac's son John was cleared of the charge that he was contemplating rebellion against the emperor and the whole affair finally had been hushed up, Alexios turned to his brother and said, "Give our mother all the news" (VIII, 8, p. 210). It is interesting to note that despite Anna Dalassena's preference for Alexios to ascend the throne, probably because of his calm disposition, nowhere does Anna suggest to the reader that Isaac ever resented or was jealous of his brother. She writes that her uncle was a perfect gentleman in word and deed and most like her own father.

More important to the development of the friendship between Isaac and Alexios was the fact that both were naturally endowed with a perceptive psychological insight which alerted them to anticipate each other's dangers and come to each other's rescue. "They were both, but Alexios more especially," Anna writes, "practiced in concealing a secret intention and a deeply laid plan by external pretences" (II, 2, p. 47). Both were well informed and knew how to manage their friends; both were adept in the art of dissimulation; both were brave to the point of endangering their own lives.

Anna notes that only in one respect were the brothers different in temperament: Isaac was rash and could become violent, while nothing could anger Alexios. Nicephoros Bryennios, who married Anna Comnena in 1097, also speaks in the same vein about his father-in-law. "He was always gay and overflowing with goodness, . . . a mixture of natural and due politeness," writes her husband, a rare gift given by Providence to humanity, a happy synthesis of these two opposing qualities. . . . He had the sweetest soul and it was almost impossible to make him angry."[51] Isaac was not at all like her father in this respect. As Anna describes him:

In an attack on an enemy, nobody ever outran Isaac, even when he was commanding a regiment, for no sooner did he see the enemy's lines than he forgot all else and hurled himself into their midst like a thunderbolt and quickly threw their men into disarray. For this reason he was captured more than once, when fighting against the Hagarenes in Asia. This characteristic of his, that he would not be restrained, is the only one worthy of censure in my uncle. (III, 3, p. 78)

Anna must surely have been annoyed over this shortcoming in her uncle, for she cites other instances of his lack of restraint. "Isaac," she observes, "was easily upset sometimes by a mere word" (VIII, 8, p. 210). Her father, on the other hand, Anna explains, while he longed for a fight and was accustomed to danger, always allowed reason to be his guide in all matters (XIII, 4, p. 332). Only once does she justify her uncle's loss of control; that occurred when Isaac's son John, Duke of Dyrrachium, was accused of hatching rebellion against the emperor. As soon as Isaac heard of this he wrote immediately to his son, informing him of the rumors that had reached him and ordering him "to resort to the Emperor with all speed." In the meantime, he himself left Byzantium and hastened to Philippopolis, where Alexios was staying, to refute the accusation made against his son. When John appeared, Isaac was relieved of his suspicions and regained his former composure, but he was filled with rage against the persons who had calumniated his son. When Isaac discovered that two of the accusers indirectly maligning his son John were his brother-in-law Melissenos and his own brother

Adrian,[52] Anna writes that "he was unable to restrain his wrath which was bubbling up again and darting a fierce look at Adrian he threatened to pull off his beard and to teach him not to try to rob the Emperor of his relations by openly telling lies about them." Alexios spoke only to tell his nephew that "out of consideration for your father, who is also my brother, I cannot bear even to hear mentioned the accusations levelled against you" (VIII, 8, 2, p. 210). He overlooked his nephew's guilt for his brother's sake.

Although Anna speaks often of the loyalty of the brothers, she forgets to tell us about one incident in the lives of the Comneni, which her husband narrates at length in his history. Isaac, who was in charge, with Alexios assisting him, had been ordered to capture the Frank Ursel who had defected with his troop of Celts. The next day Isaac learned that the Franks had fled. He entrusted Alexios with part of his troops and ordered him to go after Ursel. Before the order was even executed, scouts announced that a mass of Turks were advancing against the Roman army and were camped nearby. Isaac countermanded his order to Alexios and charged him to remain in the camp to keep the army together while he marched against the Turks with only a part of his troops. Alexios was troubled about his brother's counterorder; nevertheless, he promised to wait. Isaac met the Turks near the Cappadocian frontier, the Romans were defeated, and Isaac was captured. The Turks then marched toward the camp, and Alexios was forced to defend himself with the "fistful of men" left with him. Three days later Alexios learned of his brother's imprisonment and his need for ransom to set him free. Alexios traveled all day and night to get the needed gold, which he himself carried back to the Turks. In the meantime Isaac had escaped. When they met at Ancyra, the brothers wept for joy.[53]

But what brought Alexios and Isaac closest together was their revolt against Emperor Botaneiates in 1081. When the brothers became fully aware of the envy of Borilos and Germanos, the two Scythians who were eager to get the Comneni out of the way, the brothers, as Anna's reports, "judged it prudent to cultivate the officers of the women's apartments [in the imperial court], and through them to win in still greater measure the Queen's affection," especially since Isaac was married to Irene, the queen's cousin (II, 1, 3, p. 45). It was Isaac who approached the queen to adopt Alexios so that both brothers could visit the palace often, pay their respects to the emperor, spend a little time with him, and then go to visit the queen. Although Anna Dalassena was the chief strategist in her sons' plan to revolt, it was the fraternal amity of the brothers that helped them to outwit the menacing Borilos and Germanos. Anna proudly and honestly credits her uncle Isaac for his help to her father, but she adds that her father had helped Isaac in the arrangement of his marriage. Since her uncle's affairs had prospered so well, now Isaac desired to see Alexios succeed (II, 1, p. 45).

When Emperor Botaneiates made the mistake of choosing Synadenos as his successor instead of Constantine, the queen's son, the Comneni brothers foresaw that the queen would confide in them. Both brothers "easily guessed her secret," Anna writes, "for they were sharp-witted, shrewd, and expert in divining from a few words a man's deeply hidden and hitherto unexpressed opinion"; both "ratified their agreement by oaths," that her son Constantine should not be ousted from the empire (II, 2, p. 47).

To frustrate the schemes of Borilos and Germanos, the Comneni, who had agreed always to go to the palace together, now decided to go to the palace singly, so that "if only one were caught by the intrigues of these all-powerful Scythians, the other would escape" (II, 2, p. 48). On one occasion, when it was Isaac's turn to visit the palace and he found Alexios there, the brothers quickly adjusted to the situation. The emperor had ordered Alexios to come to the palace before the latter could notify Isaac of the change. At the table where the emperor now invited both to remain, they sat opposite each other, looking at each other, and watching all those in attendance on the emperor whom they had won over. Even the head cook, Anna says, looked on them with a friendly eye and informed Isaac of the fall of Cyzicus, the reason which summoned Alexios to the palace. Isaac in turn moved his lips slightly, and Alexios immediately sized up the situation. "Henceforward," writes Anna, "the Comneni made it their business to visit the palace and pay court to the men about the emperor even more assiduously." When the Comneni discovered that the two Scythians were planning to have them blinded, they decided that their only hope of safety lay in rebellion (II, 3, 4, pp. 48-50).

With the help of their mother, Alexios and Isaac planned all with precision. As Anna recounts the revolt, the brothers were even careful not to close the gates for fear they would creak. They brought out the horses from the stables, pretending to be carefully spreading saddle cloths for the women. The brothers escorted the women to the Forum of Constantine, took leave of them, while the women proceeded to the Church of Hagia Sophia. The Comneni returned to the royal stables, took the best horses, hamstrung the rest, and fled with all speed out of the city (II, 5, p. 53; 6, p. 55).

Anna admits with unusual candidness that her father used the utmost shrewdness to capture the throne from his brother Isaac, who was equally qualified and popular with the army. She sees no wrong in the fact that Alexios supported Isaac in his intrigues for the throne, knowing full well that, with the Ducas family behind him because of his marriage to Irene, nothing untoward to himself would result. Anna naïvely observes, "He flattered his brother in words only and made a pretense forsooth of yielding the power to him" (II, 7, pp. 59-60). In the camp at Schiza where the army acclaimed almost equally each of the brothers as the next emperor, Isaac joined the movement which came from the army and yielded graciously in favor of his brother. He arose and tried to put the red buskin on his brother's foot, but the latter refused several times, and finally Isaac cried, "Let me do it, for through you God wishes to restore the dignity of our family." Isaac reminded Alexios of the prophecy of a man who had once addressed him as "Emperor Alexios" (II, 7, p. 60).

Isaac continued to help his brother to the end of his days. "His brother Isaac whom he reverenced as a father, he made his confidant in all matters as he did his mother, and they both assisted him in the administration of the common weal," writes Anna (III, 2, p. 73). As Sebastocrator, a title which Alexios had bestowed on Isaac, he became "second Emperor," even though he did not wear the purple (III, 4, 1, p. 78). Isaac took charge of the capital in Alexios's absence (IV, 4, 1, p. 103); he raised money against the censure of the Holy Synod to help Alexios conduct his wars (V, 2, p. 118); he aided him in his struggle with heretics and rebels; in the trials of Italos, Nilos, and Basil the Bogomil, Isaac was one of the chief investigators. Indeed, despite the important assistance of the Mother of the Comneni, it is doubtful whether Alexios would have reigned as long as he did, or achieved as much as he did, had he not had his brother Isaac constantly at his side.

IV   *The Ducas Family*

She was the little daughter of Andronicos, the eldest son of the Caesar, and of illustrious lineage, for she traced her descent from the famous houses of Andronicos and Constantine Ducas. (*Alexiad,* III, 3, p. 77)

There is no question of Anna's love and reverence for the subject of her history, and yet it becomes evident early in the *Alexiad* that our porphyrogenete was her mother's daughter. The reason is plain to see: Empress Irene, who revered Anna's intellect and looked up to her husband, wanted her to succeed Alexios on the Byzantine throne; her father preferred her brother John. Irene never ceased bolstering Anna's hopes; she never stopped nagging her husband to change his mind in Anna's favor. Empress Irene, Anna, and Nicephoros Bryennios constituted a triumverate in the imperial household.

Anna never casts any discredit on her father's family; she exalts their virtues, minimizes their faults, loyally omits or underplays their acts of treason. In her history there is no full account of any family squabble among the Comneni, though the reader is aware of family intrigues in the imperial court from the plots against her father's life, some of which Anna discloses. Yet from the space she devotes to introduce us to her mother's family, it would certainly seem that she was more at home with the Ducas side of the royal household. Perhaps she championed the Ducas family because, as Demetrios Polemis asserts, they occupied a secondary social position after her father's ascension to the throne;[54] or perhaps it was because of the open hostility of the imperious Anna Dalassena for her mother Irene; or what is probably more likely, because of the loyal service of the Ducas family to Alexios. However that may be, except for her uncle Isaac and her grandmother, Anna's portrayals of the members of her father's family seem one-dimensional compared to the three-dimensional pen portraits we get of several members on her mother's side. She repeats her husband's encomium for her deceased uncle Manuel Comnenus, reputedly a great war hero. We learn from her pen that her father's brother Adrian was dignified with the title of most illustrious Protosebastos and Domestic of the West. We also learn that it was Adrian who calumniated John Comnenos, which made his father Isaac want to pull Adrian's beard. Anna informs us that Alexios gave his brother Nicephoros the rank of Great Dungaire of the fleet and then raised him to the rank of Sebasti, but we learn little else about Alexios's brothers. As for her father's sisters, Maria and Eudocia, they are not mentioned at all. About the third sister Theodora, we learn that she was the wife of the dead son of Diogenes who was being impersonated by Robert Guiscard's henchman and that after her husband's death, she followed an ascetic life and gave herself to God (X, 2, 3, p. 238).

In contrast to this, Anna gives us a number of dramatic portrayals of her mother's relatives. But what is even more revealing is that Anna writes of the origins of her mother's family, as can be noted from the quotation given above. Her husband traces the Ducas family back to the great Constantine. "The first Ducas," he narrates, "was one of those who left Rome with Emperor Constantine the Great, and by blood belonged in an authentic and legitimate manner to his illustrious sovereign. He was in effect his cousin and had received from the Emperor the dignity of Duke of Constantinople. And it is from him that all the members of the Ducas family have their name and origin."[55]

Anna must have had a close relationship with her maternal grandmother Maria, for she idealizes her origin and her beauty. She also recognized that it was her maternal grandmother who influenced her son-in-law George Palaeologos, Anna's favorite uncle, to side with the Comneni in their revolt. Bryennios writes specifically that his wife's maternal grandmother, Maria of Bulgaria, descended on her father's side from Samuel, king of the Bulgars, and on her mother's side from Contostephanos, Aballantes, and Phocas.[56] From another source, we learn that through her marriage to Andronicos, Maria became the mother of three daughters and two sons: Michael, John, Irene (Anna's mother), Anna (wife of George Palaeologos), and Theodora, who became a nun. Maria rebuilt the Church of the Chora monastery and was on close terms with Euthymios Zygabenos, author of *Dogmatic Panoply*. Prior to her death Maria took the veil and the monastic name of Xene. She died on November 21 during the reign of Alexios.[57]

All that Anna tells us about her maternal grandfather Andronicos Ducas (b. before 1045-77), who died even before Anna's parents were married, is that he was of illustrious lineage (III, 3, p. 77). Anna's husband, who refers to Andronicos as

Proedros, informs us that he was in command of the rear guard consisting of the troops of the Varangian guard and those raised by the nobles.[58] Bryennios discreetly omits the fact that Andronicos treacherously deserted Romanos IV Diogenes just before the battle of Manzikert started, which sparked the chain reaction of the mass desertions that followed.[59]

In Book IV Anna notes briefly that the porphyrogenitos Constantios, son of the former emperor Constantine X Ducas and brother of Michael Ducas, fell in battle among other prominent men. She also tells us that at his accession Michael VII Ducas took away his brothers' red shoes and their diadem and condemned them to banishment in the monastery Cyperoudes with their mother the empress Eudocia (IX, 6, p. 224). Psellos informs us that Michael VII Ducas treated his brothers well, giving them a chance to exercise imperial power with complete freedom of action. Psellos casts the blame on Nicephoros Botaneiates, for he states that it was after Michael VII's abdication that Constantine, or Constantius, was confined in a monastery by the new emperor, and that he apparently died in battle at Dyrrachium in 1082.[60]

Anna writes more fully and more warmly about Constantine Ducas (1074-c. 1095), her first fiancé, and son of Michael VII Ducas and Queen Maria. Anna was Constantine's second fiancé. As has been stated elsewhere, Anna condemned Michael for imprudently betrothing Constantine to Robert Guiscard's daughter Helen, which began the Norman hostilities. When Nicephoros ascended the throne the marriage contracts were annulled (I, 10, p. 26; 12, pp. 30, 31). Robert Guiscard used this as an excuse for war against the Romans. According to Anna, Constantine, who was only four years old at the time, "shrank from the alliance at the very outset as children do from bogeys" (I, 12, p. 33). When Emperor Botaneiates ascended the throne he took the crown from Constantine, heir apparent to the throne, then flagrantly bequeathed imperial powers to Synadenos as his successor. Anna justifiably asserts that the crown rightly belonged to Constantine through his grandfather and father (II, 2, p. 46). His mother, Empress Maria, wife of Botaneiates, made many unsuccessful attempts to have Botaneiates recognize her son as his heir. Anna reports that it was her father and her uncle Isaac who promised Constantine's mother that they would revindicate Constantine's rights to the throne. The promise was legalized in a chrysobull which made her first fiancé Alexios's partner until he lost his imperial status to her brother John (II, 2, p. 46; III, 4, pp. 79-80; VI, 8, pp. 151-52). According to Anna's husband, Constantine lost his imperial status because of a grave illness which afflicted the porphyrogenitos, thus not allowing him the strength to rule. Not long afterward, Bryennios writes, Constantine was snatched away by death.[61] Despite Anna's warm portrayal of her first fiancé, we learn nothing about his death from her pen.

Anna asks the indulgence of the reader to describe Constantine, whom she calls a "chef d'oeuvre of God's hands." Her romantic account of her royal second cousin is infused with the glow of the early years of her own youth. As usual, Anna's description is idealized. "If anyone merely looked at him, he would say that he was a descendant of the Golden Age fabled by the Greeks; so indescribably beautiful was he" (II, 12, p. 30). She adds that "he was fair-haired with a milk-white complexion" and that "his eyes were not light but gleamed under his eyebrows like those of a hawk's under a golden hood" (III, 1, p. 72).

From what Anna writes, her fiancé's loyalty to her father never wavered even after he had lost his imperial status. Constantine accompanied the emperor in his campaign against Bolcanos, who ruled over Dalmatia. When Alexios was in the region of Serres, in Macedonia, Constantine begged the emperor to be his guest at his estates, "which was very delightful and well-watered by cool, drinkable springs, and had sufficient rooms for the Emperor's reception." When the emperor prepared to leave the next morning, Constantine would not allow it until he had recovered from the fatigue of his journey (IX, 5, p. 223). Nicephoros Diogenes, who plotted to murder Alexios, tried to implicate Constantine by asking him for the loan of the steed the emperor had given him as a gift. Constantine refused on the pretext that it was impossible to give a gift of so great a value from his sovereign. From the writings of Constantine's tutor Archbishop Theophylactos of Achrida, we learn of the boy's dignity and philosophic intelligence. It seems that he loved to hunt wild animals and shoot them while on horseback.[62]

Anna writes with the same warmth about Constantine's mother, Queen Maria, daughter of King Bagrat IV (1027-72), prince of the Iberians, who had confided all her secrets to Anna during her early childhood. Recalling the unsavory rumors that coupled the name of Maria of Alania with her father, which "suggested other reasons" for her continued stay in the palace, Anna justifies the queen's stay because she feared "lest some evil should befall her son unless she first received a guarantee for his safety," and because "she was in a foreign country without kith and kin." But Anna also writes of the ribald jokes against Queen Maria. The caesar John Ducas was anxious for Maria to leave the palace. In order to allay people's unjust suspicions, the caesar advised the Queen to ask Alexios for a letter that would assure her son's safety and then leave the palace. When Alexios gave Queen Maria the chrysobull, she left the palace (III, 1, 2, pp. 71-75). Zonaras informs us that Maria lived in retirement in the Palace of Mangana, when suddenly Alexios obliged her to wear the black robe of the nun and took the red boots off her son.[63] Anna makes no mention of this.

Next to her mother, the most illustrious member of the Ducas family to arouse Anna's admiration was Caesar John Ducas (b.?-1088), her maternal great-grandfather and the only brother of Emperor Constantine X Ducas. Caesar John Ducas married Eirene, daughter of Niketas Pagonites about 1045, and by this marriage had two sons: Andronicos, father of Empress Irene, and Constantinos, both of whom he outlived.[64] A close friend of Psellos, the caesar epitomized the Byzantine feudal lord more than any other figure in the *Alexiad*. A great hunter, a cynic, resourceful, full of guile and authority, extremely wealthy with estates near Nicomedia, in Thrace, and in Bithynia, he daringly and often unscrupulously altered the destinies of several emperors, not the least of whom were Anna's parents. Buckler calls him the "Grand Old Man of the Ducas House balancing their great antagonist the imperious Mother of the Comneni."[65]

Caesar John Ducas helped his nephew Michael VII Ducas to overthrow Romanos IV Diogenes, then imprudently introduced into the palace the unscrupulous eunuch Nicephoritzes who was soon raised to the rank of *logothetes tou dromou* (director of imperial postal service). Nicephoritzes caused considerable economic disturbance because the people could no longer buy a *medimnus* of wheat with the *nomisma* but only a *medimnus* less a *pinakion* (quarter), which earned for Michael Ducas the deriding nickname of Parapinakos. When the caesar and his two sons tried unsuccessfully to get rid of Nicephoritzes, the caesar induced Michael to take the monastic habit.[66] Anna explains that the caesar did it to save Michael from being blinded, for he "knew the lightheadedness of the reigning Emperor, and feared the worst for Michael" (I, 12, p. 31). It was this Michael that Raictor impersonated and Guiscard exploited as an excuse for war.

When Michael was dethroned by Nicephoros Botaneiates, it was Caesar John Ducas who persuaded Botaneiates to marry Michael's wife Maria. Michael VII had donned the habit of a monk and was even ordained priest and archbishop of Ephesus by the patriarch of Constantinople. Previous legislation had decreed that when a spouse became a religious official the other was free to remarry.[67] Anna evidently approved of this marriage, for she explains that Queen Maria, "came from another country and had not a crowd of kinsfolk to give the Emperor trouble" (III, 2, p. 74). This shrewd move on the part of Caesar John Ducas temporarily gave him the imperial freedom he needed. In time, he fell out of favor with Emperor Botaneiates; then he donned the monastic habit to avoid being blinded.

It was really due to the efforts of Caesar John Ducas that Irene and Alexios were finally joined in marriage. In agreement with his older son Andronicos, gravely ill at the time, and with his clever daughter-in-law, the Protovestiaria Maria, Irene's mother, he arranged to unite the two most powerful families of the aristocracy by the marriage of his granddaughter Irene to the widower Alexios Comnenos.

From Irene's *Typikon* commemorating the anniversary of her father's death, we learn that Andronicos died on December 14, 1077, soon after the betrothal of Irene to Alexios. Alexios overcame his mother's opposition and married Irene Ducas sometime between November or December 1077, or possibly in January 1078, just about the time when Botaneiates ascended the throne. Irene was then thirteen years old.[68]

When Alexios and Isaac revolted in 1081, the Caesar John Ducas was living on his estate at Moroboundos. Anna gives us a dramatic account of the caesar's acceptance of her father's invitation to join the revolt. The caesar succeeded in getting his young grandsons, Michael and John, Irene's brothers, to join him, as well as a chance imperial tax collector he met on the road who was carrying a purse of gold to deliver to the capital. He also helped to convince George Palaeologos to side with Alexios. On the way to Tzouroulos, a small village of Thrace, where the

Comneni took refuge, he met a troop of Turks, and he persuaded them also to join him by promising them "much money and all kinds of rewards." To make certain that they would not leave him, he conferred their agreement by oath. After he reached Alexios and Isaac, Anna writes that the Comneni "could scarcely contain themselves for delight. Alexios went to meet him and embraced and kissed him" (II, 6, 2, p. 58). This comes as no surprise for Anna has already told us that the caesar "was marvelously glib of speech and quick in thought, and persuasion sat on his tongue as if he were a second Aeschines or Demosthenes" (II, 6, p. 57). At the caesar's suggestion they lost no time in setting out for the capital.

As has already been mentioned, Caesar John Ducas upbraided the Comneni sharply for wanting to halt to salute their mother before they reached the palace. It was also the caesar who advised Alexios to approach the Nemitzi,[69] who would more likely agree to betray the city for him. When Emperor Botaneiates sent word to the Comneni offering to adopt Alexios, if only they would let him retain the title of emperor, the Comneni were about to agree when Caesar John Ducas rushed to get to them and urged them with threats to hurry to the palace. Botaneiates made another attempt to appease the Comneni by sending Nicephoros Palaeologos, father of Anna's favorite uncle George, with the same message. This time the caesar was even more forceful. "Get away and tell the Emperor that those offers would have been more useful before the city was captured . . . tell him too, 'As you are already an old man, get off the throne and take thought for your own safety.'" Finally, on the caesar's suggestion the patriarch, a good friend of the caesar's, convinced Botaneiates to abdicate in order to prevent a civil war and bloodshed (II, 12, pp. 68-70).

Anna also writes warmly of other members of the Ducas family, all of whom served her father loyally. She praises John Ducas (c. 1064-d. before 1136), her mother's brother, the second son of Andronicos and Maria, and one of the grandsons who accompanied the caesar in the revolt of the Comneni. Alexios appointed John Ducas first Duke of Dyrrachium where he spent eleven years, then as Duke of the Fleet; for, as Anna asserts, her maternal uncle John "was exceedingly brave, skilled in warfare, and never disposed to disregard even the slightest of his orders" (VII, 8, 4, p. 186).

She writes in praise of another maternal uncle, Protostrator Michael Ducas, elder son of Andronicos and Maria, the other grandson who accompanied the caesar when the Comneni revolted. Michael succeeded in capturing Bohemond in a *"cleisura"* (a narrow pass) with all his army. "This man," writes Anna, "was celebrated for his prudence ... he was, too, very quick, and almost unrivalled in his conjecture of the future, his investigations of the actual, and in taking action accordingly" (V, 7, p. 130).

But the member of the Ducas family to whom Anna was most devoted and who influenced her life greatly was her mother Irene (1066-1133). Firstborn daughter of Andronicos and Maria, born in Constantinople, she is always referred to as Irene Doukaina, even after her marriage to Alexios.[70] Anna idealizes her mother's looks, of course. From another more objective source we learn that her mother had deep blue eyes, that her glance had unusual strength, and that she preferred to remain silent and away from the public. She blushed easily when she appeared before others besides her family.[71]

What filled Anna with fright and awe for Empress Irene was her piety. Anna recalls her mother carrying a book in her hands and poring over the writings of the didactic Fathers, especially those of the philosopher and martyr Maximus. Irene admits her own fear when she began these studies, but later she found that she could not tear herself from them. Anna had only to be patient a little, her mother advised, and she too would soon feel as she did (V, 9, 1, p. 135). Patience and piety were two virtues Anna certainly learned from her mother.

In the Preface to his *Hyle,* which Irene Doukaina asked her son-in-law to write, Bryennios praises his wife's mother who in her "high wisdom" had passed on to him "to narrate the deeds of the great Alexios."[72] Zonaras, on the other hand, writes that people approached the emperor when his wife was absent; they withdrew when she was there. According to this contemporary historian, Irene manifested a domineering and heavy-handed attitude, rebuking those who did not obey even more sharply than her husband.[73]

From what Anna writes, her mother preferred to live in her private apartments, avoiding public appearances, although this did not prevent her from devoting herself to charity. Anna refers often to her mother's bounty. On one occasion she restored to the wife of Solomon, a condemned rebel, the house which had been confiscated from him and assigned to her (XII, 6, 2, p. 313). On another occasion, when she accompanied her husband on one of his expeditions to give him the constant care he needed because of his gout, and because of the many plots which "cropped up on all sides," Irene gave free access to beggars, not only to distribute money but also to give them good advice (XII, 3, p. 307). In his poem on "The Death of Theodora," Prodromos praises Irene as "most unstinting in gifts."[74] In the case of Michael Anemas, the ringleader of a plot to kill Alexios, Anna intervened to save him from being blinded, but it was her mother who succeeded in inducing her husband to spare Michael's eyes (XII, 6, 2, pp. 313-14).

Irene's modesty and reserve are often the topic of Anna's reminiscences of her mother; her devotion to her husband appears heroic to Anna. "My mother was all in all to the ruler, my father, she was a sleepless eye at night, a most illustrious guardian by day, a good antidote to dangers at table and a salutary counter-potion to mischiefs arising from food" (XII, 3, 2, p. 306). Irene became seriously ill when she accompanied Alexios to the Chersonesus in 1112, yet we find her with him again at Philippopolis the following year.

Except for Irene's efforts to persuade her husband to select Anna as his successor, we know nothing specific of the role she played as a mother in the lives of her other children. We know from Nicetas Chionates that she loathed her son John and yearned to see him disinherited. She even entered into conspiracy to have him assassinated so that Anna and her husband could succeed Alexios on the throne.[75]

One of Irene's last acts to her memory was the establishment of the monastery of Kecharitomene ("all gracious") for the use of imperial women; she had it erected next to her husband's monastery Philanthropos ("lover of humanity"). The charter of the foundation, the *Typikon*, drawn up and signed in purple by the empress "Irene, in the Lord Christ, faithful Queen of the Romans," is preserved in the Bibliothèque Nationale in Paris with the number 384.[76] In founding her convent, Irene had in mind its eventual use for herself and her family. It was there that Anna Comnena went after the death of her husband in 1138, and there too went Anna's daughter, who had been widowed quite young and who was also named Irene Ducas. Anna writes nothing about Kecharitomene in her *Alexiad,* and yet nowhere is her mother's sense of *philanthropia* seen to greater advantage. Among other stipulations she orders that on Christmas Day two *modia* and four *nomismata* were to be given to each suppliant at the gateway of the monastery. Irene insisted that bread, wheat, and leftovers of meals be distributed daily to the poor.[77] Irene's monastery maintained distributions of food to the poor and also adopted orphan girls who were educated there. Furthermore, she left a request in her testament that upon her death and the death of her husband, the monastic community make more distributions than usual.[78]

Originally, the protection of the convent was entrusted to Irene's daughter Eudocia, who had made an unfortunate marriage and had become a nun after her husband was turned out of the palace; she died there prematurely in 1120. Irene herself then assumed the position of protector which at her death would pass on successively first to her favorite daughter Anna, then to her second daughter Mary, followed by her granddaughter Irene Ducas. It was then to be transmitted from generation to generation to the female descendants of Anna Comnena. There Empress Irene, or Xene, retired; there she lived until her death on February 19, 1133.[79] She had outlived her husband by fourteen years, six months and four days.

V *Anna, Princess Porphyrogenete*

He found his wife in the pangs of childbirth, in the room which had of old been set apart for the Empresses' confinements, our forefathers called it the 'purple' room, and from it the name 'Porphyrogeniti' [born in the purple] has become current in the world. (*Alexiad,* VI, 8, pp. 150-51)

Anna Comnena was born on Saturday, December 2, 1083, and looked exactly like her father; she had the same dark eyes, the same dark skin. Georgios Tornikes, metropolitan of Ephesus and Anna's intimate friend in her later life, has left us an interesting pen portrait of Anna, in his recently published funeral oration. In this fifty-page encomium, he tells us:

Her large eyes . . . radiating a restrained joy . . . were endowed with a lively and easy movement when glancing around her but most often were steady and calm. Her eyebrows were like a rainbow; her nose was slightly curved towards the lips . . . edged like a rose-blossom. The whiteness of her skin was tinged with a rosiness which gave color to her cheeks up to her old age. Her face was a perfectly chiseled circle. . . . Her shoulders even . . . her limbs were agile and beautiful. . . . Her body was like a lyre or like a well-harmonized guitar, a fine instrument for a fine soul.[80]

According to her own story, Anna's birth was marked by a singular event. Four days before her birth, Empress Irene felt labor pains. She made the sign of the cross on her womb, saying, "Wait a little, child, for your father's coming!" Irene's mother rebuked her daughter saying, "How do you know whether he will come within a month? And how will you be able to bear the pains so long?" But Alexios returned to the capital on the day of Anna's birth after having defeated the Norman invaders. Anna saw in this divine hearing of Empress Irene's order a prediction of the great love she would have for her parents (VI, 8, p. 151). But what is of great importance to Anna, and she never lets the reader forget it, is that she was "born in the purple" which bestowed upon her the title of Porphyrogenete.

Anna's birth, which naturally delighted her parents, was followed with the traditional rites observed at the birth of a princess. But since Anna was also the firstborn child, she was immediately acclaimed successor to the throne. As she herself tells us, after a few days had passed her parents honored her with a crown and royal diadem (VI, 8, p. 151). She was honored further when her parents affianced her to Constantine Ducas, the seven-year-old son of Queen Maria and the dethroned Emperor Michael Ducas. At the time of her birth, Constantine, who was also her mother's second cousin, ruled as coemperor with her father, wore a tiara, was acclaimed second in all acclamations, as she too was now acclaimed (VI, 8, p. 151).

She enjoys recalling what some of her relatives and her mother must have repeated many times, that "the leaders of the acclamation shouted out 'Constantine and Anna' together at the time for acclamations" which continued for a long time. This joint acclamation symbolized for Anna what was to befall her later, though she admits that she cannot tell whether it can be called good or ill fortune (VI, 8, pp. 151-52).

Despite the lapse of more than half a century, the memory of her first fiancé presents a romantic side to Anna's nature not often seen in her history. From her own statements, we see that the earliest years of this imperially-minded little girl were as sweet as any child could desire. She was proud to be a porphyrogenete, very proud of being acclaimed successor to the throne, and affianced to so handsome a nobleman as Constantine.

VI   *Birth of John Porphyrogenitos*

The child had a swarthy complexion, broad forehead, lean cheeks, a nose neither snub nor acquiline but something between the two, very black eyes which betokened, as far as one can judge from an infant's face, a quick intelligence. (*Alexiad*, VI, 8, p. 152)

From what Anna says, when Maria Porphyrogenete was born a little more than three years after her own birth, showing "signs of virtue and wisdom which were to distinguish her later," her parents "much desired to have a son as well and their prayer was granted" (V, 8, p. 152). John Porphyrogenitos was born on the eleventh indiction or sometime between September 1, 1087 and August 31, 1088.

Anna's unflattering description of her brother, except for his very black eyes, would probably not have been open to so much criticism from Byzantine historians were it not so marked a contrast to her descriptions of other members of her family whom she generally idealizes equally in almost a hyperbolic monochrome of ideal beauty. It was true that John Porphyrogenitos was not a good-looking baby; others have written about his "ugliness and dark coloring."[81] When we consider how the event of John's birth had altered Anna's destiny so drastically, her brief statement about his birth, quoted above, is remarkably objective and relatively free of the jealousy that she actually felt for John, since his birth removed her from accession to the throne. Her remarks on the joy of parents, and even about those who "feigned delight," do not necessarily pertain to her own feelings; she would hardly be subjective about his birth at the end of her life, when he too had been dead for five years. She writes:

Thereupon my parents were indeed overjoyed and no trace of sadness remained, as their desire had been fulfilled. The whole populace too rejoiced, seeing their masters so happy, and congratulated each other and were delighted. Then you would have seen the palace full of rejoicing and no shadow of sorrow or even care, for all the well-disposed rejoiced from the bottom of their heart, whilst the others feigned delight. . . . However on this one occasion universal joy could be witnessed, as one and all were really pleased. (VI, 8, p. 152)

She records the fact of John's acclamation without mentioning her own loss of succession to the throne. "As my parents naturally wished to raise the child to the rank of Emperor and leave him the Empire of the Romans as his inheritance," she writes, "they deemed him worthy of being baptized and crowned in the great Church of God." She adds wistfully, as if to round out the sorrows which had warped her life, "This is what happened to us children 'born in the purple' from the very starting point of our birth" (VII, 8, p. 152).

There is no question that it was hatred for her brother which inspired her to leave him out of her *Alexiad*, except where it was factually necessary to include his name. Later events certainly proved this when she even attempted his assassination. Yet writing her history when she was sixty-five years old, thirty years after the death of her father, "keeping herself in a corner and occupying herself with books and God," bereft of her mother, her favorite brother Andronicos, and her adored caesar, it is hard to imagine how she could have felt otherwise. So far as is known, she and John were never reconciled. The reader must bear in mind that her purpose in writing the *Alexiad*, as she says in her Preface, was to recount the deeds done by her father. She fulfilled that purpose. To be sure, had she given John importance in the *Alexiad*, she would have filled a gap in Byzantine history, but her own history would not have been the panegyric of her father which the *Alexiad* is. She knew only too well that her father wanted John to succeed him. This was the bitter cup she had to drink, loving her father as much as she did. She could not allow John's visage to blur her purpose. In a sense the *Alexiad* is Anna's sublimation for having been denied the rule of Byzantium when she was so innately equipped to be a sovereign. Morally speaking, the *Alexiad* is Anna's atonement and her redemption.

CHAPTER 3

Education of a Byzantine Princess

I *Her Early Life at Court*

For from childhood, from eight years upwards, I was brought up
with the Queen, and as she conceived a warm affection for me she
confided all her secrets to me. (*Alexiad,* III, 1, p. 72)

THE queen referred to in the above quotation is Maria of
Alania, mother of Constantine Ducas, Anna's seven-year-old
royal cousin, to whom she was officially betrothed soon after her
birth. As was the custom of the time, the princess was
immediately placed in the care of her fiancé's mother, the twice-
married exotically lovely Queen Maria, daughter of Iranian
nomads, who was still living in the "Upper" palace, also called
Boucoleon, with her son. After Alexios's succession to the throne,
Empress Irene and Queen Maria shared in Anna's upbringing for
the first eight years of her life.

The author of the *Alexiad* recalls those early years in her life
with nostalgia, sorrow, and compassion, for the woman whom she
was taught to regard as her future mother-in-law. The beauty and
personality of Queen Maria must surely have been a delightful
change for Anna, imperially indoctrinated by her grandmother
in an atmosphere that had "somewhat the appearance of a holy
monastery" (III, 8, 1, p. 86).

But this divinely happy environment of great expectations for
Anna as a future empress and as the wife of her royal second
cousin lasted only until she was nine years old. In 1092, Constantine Ducas lost his imperial status to her brother John, and
she herself lost her rights of succession. This was Anna's first
traumatic experience, which, judging from later events, never
healed. Her second traumatic experience followed on the heels of
the first, when she was removed from the care of Queen Maria
and returned to the care of her father. Had Anna's relationship
with her intended mother-in-law continued unbroken, our blue-
stocking historian might have lost some of the bitterness and

hatred she felt for her brother John. Her third traumatic
experience came three years later. Anna was eleven years old
when Constantine died. She sincerely felt the loss of her first
fiancé; it is difficult to understand why she says nothing of any
illness or of the causes of his death.

Reliving those early years and once again envisioning Queen
Maria, whose beauty and confidences had warmed Anna's heart,
and recalling her handsome first fiancé, our porphyrogenete
exudes in her writing the happiness of an impressionable little
girl living in the best of all possible worlds. After that, life in
the court for the regally-oriented Anna, who had all the makings
of an empress, was stripped of that early fairy-tale glamor. "I
was only eight years old when my misfortunes began," she
explains as she contemplates sadly the loss of these early, care-
free, joyful years.

II   Her Education and Training

I was not ignorant of letters, for I carried my study of Greek to
the highest pitch, and was also not unpracticed in rhetoric; I perused
the works of Aristotle and the dialogues of Plato carefully, and
enriched my mind by the "quaternion" of learning.[1] (Alexiad, Preface, I, p. 1)

Nowhere in the Alexiad do we get a more three-dimensional
portrait of Anna than when she is writing of her father's contribution to learning and the advancement of education. In a very
real sense, her greatest identity with the subject of her history is
in their mutual dedication to intellectual, religious, and cultural
pursuits. For Anna, education made the man even more than
noble birth.

Anna focuses sharply her father's contribution in this field of
Byzantine life from the moment he ascended the throne. He
encouraged those who were inclined to learning, but "bade them
prefer the study of sacred writings to Greek literature" (V, 9,
p. 136).

Her estimation of the importance of education is further high-
lighted in her evaluation of the several personages who helped
or hindered the advancement of learning during her father's
reign. Her keenest admiration is for Michael Psellos, widely
recognized for his encyclopedic learning; Psellos was thoroughly
acquainted with Greek and Chaldean literature and had grown

famous in his time for his wisdom (V, 8, p. 133). When she writes of Euthymios Zygabenos, whom her father had commissioned to write *Dogmatic Panoply* in order to explain all heresies, she considers it essential for the reader to know that Zygabenos was not only the best authority on ecclesiastical dogma but that he had "pursued his grammatical studies very far, and was not unversed in rhetoric" (XV, 9, p. 415). Anna, who was not untrained in mathematics, discusses geometry with Diogenes because his knowledge of the subject was so keen he could feel "the figures made in solid material (or in relief). For by feeling these all over with his hands he gained comprehension of all the theorems and figures of geometry" (IX, 10, 2, p. 233).

So strongly does Anna feel about the importance of teachers and formal education that she actually believes that the lack of formal schooling was a basic cause of the heresy that was mushrooming all over Byzantium during her father's reign. In her judgment, Leo, bishop of Chalcedon, who voted against her father's appropriation of unused church treasures to help finance the war, "was incapable of making a precise statement with conviction as he was absolutely untrained in the science of reasoning" (V, 2, p. 119). In the case of Italos, she relates his heretical teaching to the fact that "this man had not studied very much under learned professors. . . . he was never able to plumb the depths of philosophy for he was of such a boorish and barbarous disposition that he could not endure teachers even when learning from them" (V, 8, p. 133). Although she admits that Nilos, another heretic, had studied the writings of the saints very closely, yet she feels that he went astray about the meaning of the writings because he had never learned the art of reasoning. "He was quite uninitiated into Hellenic culture," she writes, "and never even had a teacher who might from the start have explained to him the deep meanings of the Divine writings" (X, 1, p. 235).

Although Anna's evaluation of these men appears limited, it cannot be denied that she was well trained to recognize the difference between the dilettante and the true intellectual. Aside from the abundant classical and biblical allusions strewn familiarly throughout her history, which in themselves testify to Anna's erudition, we have the testimony of three Byzantine contemporary writers who recognized Anna's superior intellect and her culture. In his poem on the "Death of Theodora" (Anna's daughter-in-law), Theodore Prodromos calls Anna "Porphyrogen-ite Caesarissa Kyra Anna Dukaina and a shoot of the Ducas stem," and again "wise Anna, absolute intellect, home of the graces."[2] In the *Epithalamium* by the same author, he calls Anna "Fourth Grace" and "Tenth Muse."[3] Zonaras, who wrote his *Epitome Historion* about the same time Anna wrote her *Alexiad*, goes so far as to say that Anna surpassed the education of her literary husband because of her keenness of mind and her associa-tion with learned men. "His wife pursued education in letters not less, if not more than himself and had a tongue that atticized accurately and a keenest mind towards the height of theorems."[4] Nicetas Chionates, another contemporary historian, whose *History of John Comnenos* is a primary source for the reign of Anna's brother, Emperor John II, refers to Anna as "the Caesarissa Anna who had received the broadest education and was versed in all the sciences and in philosophy."[5] Georgios Tornikes speaks of Anna as "a woman who had attained the highest summit of wisdom, both secular and divine, manifesting around her the grandeur of a celestial intelligence."[6]

Once her tutors had "hellenized the tongue" of their pre-cocious pupil in reading, writing, and grammar, they advanced her to the study of the classics, rhetoric, science, philosophy, and the "quaternion" of learning (see note 1, p. 165). In Anna's grief-stricken awareness that the poets no longer receive even second-ary attention, she reveals the depth of her own learning when she writes:

I myself spent so much time over the same things. And when I was released from that childish teaching and betook myself to the study of rhetoric and touched on philosophy and in between these sciences turned to the poets and historians, by means of these I polished the roughness of my speech, then with the aid of rhetoric I felt that the highly complex complications of grammatical parsing were to be condemned. (XV, 7, pp. 411-12)

Anna refers here to the science of schedography which Psellos had restored but which Anna seems to have hated. It was the art of minute grammatical analysis and parsing, a didactive method used to interpret unusual grammatical forms, rare words, and the like, in ancient or religious texts, which gave greater im-portance to the grammar than it did to the literature.[7]

In her discussion of those subjects which occupied the attention of our historian, there is no evidence that Anna had any interest in Latin. Indeed, she goes to some trouble to justify her occasional use of the names of the Normans. "Let no one find fault with me," she writes, "for introducing these barbaric names which are a stain on the style of my history; for not even Homer disdained to mention Boetians and certain barbarian islands for the sake of accuracy in his history" (X, 8, p. 254). It would certainly seem that Anna cared little about Latin, if she knew any at all.

In the *Alexiad*, written in "atticizing" Greek, Anna never refers specifically to any formal school education; there are no girls' schools mentioned anywhere in Byzantine history. "Of the facilities for female education we know nothing," writes Runciman.[8] One can assume, therefore, that Anna was educated by private tutors as all children of royalty were at that time.

We get an inkling of Anna's independence of mind from the funeral oration, delivered by Georgios Tornikes, sometime after her death. Tornikes explains that Anna was trained in virtue by her parents, but not in secular culture. They allowed her to study science and literature, so long as it could be related to the divine and contribute to her moral education; her parents were strongly opposed to Anna's study of grammar and poetry which could not be Christianized, and was morally neutral. Tornikes justifies her parents' opposition to secular culture because "they suspected it of being insidious, and because the absence of culture in her parents threw into relief the genius of their daughter."[9] It is all the more remarkable to read that at the age of thirteen, Anna outwitted her parents and took lessons in grammar from one of the palace eunuchs without the knowledge of her parents. Later, her mother consented to her study of grammar.[10]

From what Anna herself reveals to us of her intellectual pursuits, her three lifelong interests were the classics, highly popularized by the Comneni; the Bible, which took priority over all other studies in Byzantine Greece; and medicine, for which Anna had unusual aptitude. She was uniquely dedicated to broad intellectual and cultural pursuits throughout her life; in the main, however, it is her extensive and intensive learning in these three areas which molded her moral precepts, her philosophy of life, and her approach to history.

Her most thorough education was in the classics, which Anna quotes with enviable familiarity. From Anna's direct statement quoted at the beginning of this section, we learn that she perused the works of Aristotle and the dialogues of Plato, from whose works she learned "the very essence of Hellenism." According to Buckler, who made a detailed study of Anna's literary allusions in her own scholarly work, *Anna Comnena*, our Greek princess has nine references to Aristotle and his teaching, eleven to Plato and his followers, forty-seven to the *Iliad*, seven to the *Odyssey*, ten to both, and two which are composite. Buckler believes that on the whole Anna quotes Homer with greater accuracy than the Bible.[11]

In an interesting analysis on Anna's classical learning, Radislav Katičič asserts that Anna's epic spirit arises from the mentality of the great feudal lords of Byzantium. "The classic rhetoric in the *Alexiad*," writes Katičič, "vibrates genuine epic impulse, but it is an extreme personal epic disposition.... The epic character of Anna's writing does not arise either from an oratorical construction of the word, or from a narrative character of the work, but from an inner disposition and the manner of thought of the writer."[12] It would seem, then, that Anna's epic spirit is not humanistic; rather, it is a Byzantine Christianized adaptation of the pagan epic of ancient Greece.

Tornikes analyzed Anna's Byzantine Christianized approach to the classics somewhat differently. According to Tornikes, Anna tempered the wisdom of the ancients with the wisdom inspired by God. Anna refused to accept Aristotle's theory that the universe had no beginning, thus reducing the world to automatism. For Anna the Good is the essence, and the One is identified with Being, who is God, the principal creator of all things. Anna does not accept Aristotle's theory of entelechy, which states that everything in the world has its own end, that it has its own potential, and that when it reaches its potential it reaches its perfect completeness or entelechy. According to Aristotle's doctrine of entelechy the soul of man dies and our universe is therefore withdrawn from Providence. For Anna the soul is divine, immortal and incorruptible. Tornikes states that he often discussed philosophy with Anna.[13]

In keeping with the intensity which the Byzantines felt about their religion, especially demonstrated by Alexios, who gave priority to theology and the sacred writings over all other studies during his reign, it would seem that Anna was more deeply concerned about the practices of religion than the other two areas of her greatest interest. Certainly, she is unusually knowledgeable on the subject when she is discussing heresy. Her many observations on the nature and behavior of people, the events of her father's reign, and even the topography of the land which her father selects strategically for his encampments, and which she often describes, are colored in a measure by her sense of piety which actually sets the tone of her book and predominates throughout. Her sense of forgiveness, her kindness, her philanthropy are all rooted in her upbringing as a devout Greek Orthodox Christian. Although her battle scenes are spectacularly replete with the goriest details, she criticizes generals who "rejoice in blood," and who "ever welcome fighting rather than peace." She admires men who are generous and are ever ready to give; "true liberality," she writes, "is not as a rule judged by the quantity of money supplied, but is weighed by the spirit of the giver" (II, 4, p. 52). She admires "men of firm disposition who can fix their mind on the matter before them and overlook disturbances" (II, 9, p. 63). She detests oath-breaking.

From her childhood to the completion of her *Alexiad,* Anna occupied herself "with books and God" (XIV, 7, 3, p. 382). In almost every page of her history there is some mention of Divine Providence. In the Preface she writes of her natural zeal for learning as "gifts which God apportioned to her at birth." When the captured rebel Bryennios passed up an opportunity to kill her father, it was "God was guarding the Comnenos, like a precious object, for a greater dignity, intending by means of him to restore the fortune of the Romans" (I, 6, 5, p. 20). She praises her aunt Theodora, who after her husband's death in battle, "embraced a solitary life and followed an ascetic life most strictly and devoted herself entirely to God" (X, 2, p. 238). When Bohemond sues for peace Alexios does not reject his proposals, despite the many times the Norman had deceived the Emperor, because "divine law of the gospel commands Christians to forgive each other all offences" and because "it is better to be deceived than to offend God and to transgress divine laws" (XIII, 8, 2, p. 343). In the ten-page treaty, which Anna records verbatim, that ended the long-standing enmity between Alexios and Bohemond, our historian remembers to add that the treaty was signed by "the hand of the bishop of Amalfi, most dear to God, who had come to the Emperor as ambassador from

the Pope" (XIII, 12, 4, p. 357). When Alexios is arranging his
lines and phalanxes in battle array, Anna says that her father
"looked upon it as an arrangement directly inspired by God
and a marshalling due to the angels" (XV, 3, 2, p. 398).

According to Buckler, Anna has eighty-seven biblical references
in the fifteen books of the *Alexiad;* there are two references to the
Apocrypha, forty to the Old Testament, thirteen of which are to
the Psalms, and forty-five to the New Testament. Seventeen are
allusions to biblical personages.[14]

Anna had unusual aptitude for medicine. The *Alexiad* is amply
strewn with her suggestions for home remedies and practical
nursing, probably known to many illiterate mothers in Byzantine
Greece; however, she shows more than practical nursing
experience when she diagnoses the causes of her father's gout and
his last illness. She informs us that his gout was caused by an
injury to his leg while playing polo, to which her father gave
superficial attention; this neglect drew the rheumatics to the
injured part, which was worsened by his "immense sea of worries" into which the Franks had engulfed him and left him
exhausted.

During her father's last illness, she refers respectfully to the
several doctors attending her father as "the disciples of
Aesclepios," although she differs from them in their treatment
and boldly offers her own diagnosis and treatment to which they
listen as if she were a colleague. Anna proudly admits that she
was there by order of her mother "to adjudge the physicians'
arguments" since not all were in agreement in their diagnosis
and treatment of the disease which afflicted her father. She
nursed her father diligently with the food which she herself
prepared and served to him daily; she watched the movements
of her father's pulse and studied his respiration. Her mother
often looked steadfastly at her and waited for her "oracular
decision as she had been wont to do at other critical moments."
It was Anna rather than the doctors who recognized that "the
pulse in her father's arteries had finally stopped" (XV, 11, 4
pp. 425-26).

Anna's piety unquestionably imbued her spirit with lofty moral
values; she was knowledgeable in many areas of learning; and
from the testimony of contemporary writers, we can say that
she was truly the most cultured woman of her age. As a
distinguished member of the feudal aristocracy, she also reflects

some of the superstitions current at the imperial court, which unfortunately mar her objective analysis of her father's reign. For example, although she admits that Alexios attributed comets to natural causes, she justifies his acceptance of the meaning of the appearance of a comet from a vision seen by Basileios, prefect of Byzantium, that foretells the movement of the Franks and their destruction (XII, 4, p. 308). Again, Anna tells us that her uncle, who during their revolt was equally acclaimed emperor by the army, conceded the throne to his brother because of a prophecy once addressed to him by a man near Carpianum (II, 7, p. 60). In her father's battle against Bohemond at Larissa, Anna feels it important to mention that her father was assured of victory through a vision he saw in his sleep which told him that he would conquer (V, 5, p. 127). Anna's use of visions and dreams to explain the history of her subject's reign certainly weakens the objective evaluation which she is so anxious to maintain throughout.

Byzantine scholars have criticized Anna for upholding her father's use of ruse and trickery to gain a campaign, to win the throne, to combat heresy. She finds praiseworthy her father's "new plan which was by flattery and promise to suborn some of the guards on the walls, and by thus stealing, so to say, their goodwill, to capture the city" (II, 9, p. 63). Anna justifies her father's tactics because to her "it has always seemed best to carry out some wily, yet strategic, move even during the battle itself, whenever one's army is not adequate compared with the strength of one's opponents" (XV, 3, pp. 395-96). Most of all, Anna supports her father's trickery to get Basil the Bogomil to incriminate himself. She tells us that Alexios had invited Basil "on some righteous pretext," even rose from his chair to greet him, sat by him, and shared his table, pretending that he wanted to become his disciple, "to effect his soul's salvation," and thus trapped the Bogomil monk, which led him to the stake (XV, 8, 1, pp. 412-13).

But in evaluating Anna's moral sense, we must keep in mind her position as a member of the landowning, military aristocracy of Byzantium. Her evaluation of her father's deeds naturally reflects the standards of that class. As a Byzantine princess living in the imperial court, Anna was fully aware that other powerful members of the military aristocracy were intriguing for the Byzantine throne. She knew the trickery and ruse used by the foreign enemies of Byzantium battering almost at the very gates of the capital, threatening the very existence of the Greek Empire. It is important to remember, too, that the fanatic religious zeal of the military aristocracy to combat heresy, was, in a very real sense, a tactical weapon in the hands of its rulers for the perpetuation of feudalism, which Anna was certainly not out to destroy.

In evaluating Anna's education and training which shaped her character and personality, we must also take into account her loss of succession to the throne which altered the course of her life so drastically. The humorless cast of her mind mantling her history can be attributed in some measure to this unfortunate event, which she regarded as a blight on her life. Not tempered by either education or religious training was her lifelong and bitter hatred of her brother and her plot to assassinate him.

III   *Death of her Fiancé; Marriage*

My lawful husband was the Caesar Nicephoros, a scion of the clan of the Bryennii. (*Alexiad*, Preface, 3, p. 2)

As has already been stated, Constantine Ducas, Anna's first fiancé, died when she was eleven years old. Early in 1097, when Anna was fourteen years old, she was married to Nicephoros Bryennios, who was three years her senior. Like herself, he too was a member of a powerful military, landowning family, but the Bryennii did not enjoy the same high social status of the Comneni.[15] In the Prologue to her Will, Anna states that she had hoped to remain single and that she married to please her father.[16] She expresses no such opinion in her *Alexiad;* and from the excessive praise of her husband, it would seem that she was proud to belong to the Bryenni clan.

Most critics agree that Alexios selected Nicephoros Bryennios to be his son-in-law for political reasons; it was a piece of diplomacy on the part of the emperor to appease the partisans of the elder rebel Bryennios, whom he had captured. Anna herself supplies a clue when she writes that, at the time of her father's revolt, all the men from the country towns flocked to Alexios as volunteers and proclaimed him emperor; the only exception were the men of Oresteias, who had an old grudge against him for having captured Bryennios (II, 6, p. 58). It is possible, as Byzantine scholars believe, that Alexios hoped to appease these men through Anna's marriage.

There seems to be a difference of opinion among Byzantine scholars concerning the Bryenni family. Anna herself tells us that the man she married was the grandson of the rebel Bryennios, Great Domestic of the West, from 1068 to 1071, and the son of that Bryennios who once aimed at the throne and had himself done the same and been deprived of his eyes (X, 2, p. 240). Buckler accepts Seger's statement that the son-in-law of Alexios was the son, not the grandson, of Alexios's old enemy and quotes Theophylactos who addressed the ex-rebel as the *sympetheros* (relative by marriage) of Alexios.[17] Zonaras definitely gives the relationship as that of father and son and adds that the father of Alexios's enemy was also blinded in 1057.[18] According to Henri Grégoire, Buckler and Zonaras are wrong and Anna Comnena is right. Grégoire explains that in 1078, the son of Nicephoros the rebel was about sixteen years of age, and his father, born in 1062, would have been thirty-five years old at the time of Anna's marriage when she was only fifteen; he would have been fifty-four years old in the battle of 1116, the last campaign of Alexios against the Turks.[19] Anna writes that her husband Nicephoros

noticed the battle in the rear, and longed ardently to go to the assistance of the men at the back, but as he did not wish to prove his inexperience or his youth he restrained his raging anger against the barbarians and continued to march on in good order and the same formation. (XV, 5, pp. 402-3)

Anna could not have written about "inexperience or youth" of the older Bryennios. Grégoire concludes that whatever Anna's ignorance on certain subjects may have been, she must naturally have known better than anyone else if her husband was the son or the grandson of the elder Bryennios.[20] According to Anna then, Nicephoros, who had plenary jurisdiction over Adrianople in 1094, was the son of that Bryennios who had formerly revolted and was blinded. He was one of the chiefs of the conspiracy of 1067 who put Emperor Isaac on the throne. The Bryennios whom her father captured was the grandfather of the Nicephoros Anna married in 1097.

IV *Married Life*

For everything, strength, swiftness, physical beauty, in fact all good qualities of mind and body combined to adorn this man. (*Alexiad,* VII, 2, p. 170)

Anna's married life lasted forty years; from the many laudatory references to her husband, it must have been a happy marriage. Nicephoros was dedicated to his intellectual wife; she looked up to him as her ideal. He was attractive and had a graceful figure. "To look at him," his wife writes, "or to listen to him was a pure delight.... He was most remarkable in every way." He was a man "who far outshone his contemporaries by his surpassing beauty, his superior intelligence, and his accurate speech" (Preface, 3, p 2). She praises her husband for his piety, his humanity, his skill in archery, especially on that Holy Thursday of April 2, 1097. She was a young bride when her father sent her husband out to defend Constantinople against the unforeseen attack of the crusaders camped under the walls of the city (X, 9, p. 259). In that battle, Anna tells us, her "Caesar's bow was in every deed the bow of Apollo" (X, 9, p. 260). He held high positions in her father's campaigns. Anna's father must have been enormously pleased to have a son-in-law like Nicephoros Bryennios.

Highlighting Anna's married life were the intellectual pursuits both had in common. "He read every book and applied himself to every branch of learning (VII, 2, pp. 170-71). "He wrote several excellent monographs even during times of stress and trouble" (Preface, 3, p. 2). She was proud of his writing. According to her, his style had harmony and grace, but what she regarded as his greatest achievement was the history of her father's reign that he had started to write by order of Empress Irene, partly to please his mother-in-law, and partly because his own feelings about Alexios were so deep that he could not allow himself to "pass over his deeds in silence, so that they would perish in the abyss of forgetfulness." However, he modestly admits that his work is not a history but material for a history.[21] According to his wife, Nicephoros was designated to write the history of her father not only because of his natural gifts but also because of his "accurate understanding of affairs ... his knowledge of literature and his varied acquaintance with both native and foreign learning!" (Preface, 4, p. 4). Anna shows her high regard for the partial *Hyle Historias* her husband had written before his untimely death by referring the reader to it on five different occasions.

What must have added considerable interest to their lives were the polar differences in their dispositions. Nicephoros Bryennios seems to have been a calm person, not nearly as nervous or ambitious as his wife; his calmness of spirit, except for that one instance when her husband failed her in the plot to have her brother assassinated, must surely have soothed her turbulent soul. Anna speaks often of her husband's persuasiveness and his oratory. She is delighted to recall how her father called on him to calm the rebellious Gregory Taronites (XII, 7, p. 316). A short time after her father had honored her husband with the rank of Panhypersebastos, the stubborn Bohemond called on him to serve as moderator between Alexios and himself during the drawing up of their final treaty. Anna must have enjoyed recalling that her husband "took Bohemond by the hand and led him back to the Emperor" (XIII, 11, p. 348). Alexios even called on his son-in-law to stem the tide of heresy at Philippopolis; it was his father-in-law who had trained him in the study of sacred books (XIV, 8, p. 386).

Empress Irene also loved and respected the abilities of her son-in-law, for she called on him whenever she acted as regent for Alexios and needed help, which Zonaras believes is the reason her son John feared him.[22] Nicetas Chionates, writing about Irene's preference for Nicephoros as a successor to the throne over her own son John states:

At times she would introduce the name of Bryennios into the discussion, on whom she would lavish all sorts of praise, describing him as most capable in getting things done and as a man of liberal education which does indeed have an ennobling and orderly effect on character and is of no small help to future rulers who wish to establish a safe form of government.[23]

We learn nothing either from Anna or from her husband's unfinished history about their domestic life or about their role as parents, other than the few words Anna says in the Preface, that her husband was anxious about his family while he was on campaigns, which probably kept him away from home often and for long stretches of time. We do get an inkling about their home life from the *Epithalamium* of Prodromos, who tells us that Anna had two sons. One was called Alexios, who took his mother's surname; the other was named John Ducas, who took his grandmother's maiden name. Both boys received their education under the direction of their mother. From the same source we learn that Anna's two sons had learned to ride, play polo, hunt, and set phalanxes in array.[24]

We get an inkling of Anna as a mother and as a wife from the
Prologue to her Will, which she says she wrote to please her
mother. She writes of her joy in her husband and her very
handsome and fine children. She mentions the fact that she lost
some children, "which was the will of God"; others survived, she
tells us, and she hopes that they may go on living. One other
item pertaining to Anna's married life is found in the Prologue
to her Will. She boasts of the "best and divinest husband under
the sun . . . in descent and virtue, in both body and soul,
endowed to the highest degree."[25]

Empress Irene's *Typikon* mentions that Anna and Nicephoros
had two daughters; one was named Irene Ducas; no name is
given for the other. Both of Anna's daughters succeeded their
mother and grandmother in the patronage of the Kecharitomene
convent founded by Empress Irene.[26] We know from Prodromos
that one of her daughters-in-law was named Theodora.[27] For
the story of Anna's other daughter-in-law, Zonaras informs us
that she was sent to Constantinople in the last year in the life
of Alexios and was with the other members of the family around
his deathbed. He does not mention her by name.[28]

When we reflect carefully on Anna's remarks about her husband, we discover that she praises him for his literary achievements, his bravery or skill in his military campaigns, or in some
other service for her father, or, as at the very end of his life, to
list the campaigns he fought with her brother John during his
reign. We know from Anna that her husband's illness may have
been caused in part by "his overwhelming anxiety" about his
family, but she tells us nothing specific about Nicephoros as a
husband or as a father. Obviously, she felt that her private life
had no place in a history of her father.

CHAPTER 4

A House Divided

I Role of Anna at Court

And as a rule I was with my father and mother and accompanied them. For it was not my lot to be kept at home and brought up in the shade and in luxury. (*Alexiad*, XIV, 7, 2, p. 381)

ANNA lived at the Boucouleon palace from the time of her birth in 1083 to the year of her father's death in 1118. Yet, from the scant information she gives us, we can only surmise what her role at court must have been. From the three already mentioned contemporary Byzantine writers—Prodromos, Nicetas Chionates, and Zonaras—we know that the aristocracy of the court admired Caesarissa Anna for her scintillating intellect even more than they did her respected, scholarly husband. She must surely have participated in discussions in astrology, science, and geometry with the scholars who frequented the court. She surely entered into discussions on the subject of heresy with the monks who were always to be seen at her grandmother's table. From her own often-repeated avowals of devotion to her parents and her mother's "oracular" dependency on her knowledge, we can also assume that Anna must have been consulted about some of the events that took place at the imperial court, which she describes vividly in the *Alexiad*. As a woman of culture, her father must have relied on his eldest daughter to serve as official hostess at banquets to which dignitaries or foreign potentates were invited. From her dramatic delineations of the personages who came to the court, her father's diplomatic handling of the rude Franks, especially Bohemond, whose covetous eye was on the Byzantine throne, one gets the impression that Anna was not left out of any of the comings and goings in the palace. She herself tells us that the women's quarters were separated by only a curtain, which made it easy for her to hear what was taking place in the court. This is how she heard her father's and Isaac's investigation of Basil the Bogomil, which she records in such detail after so many years. And then, from the quotation given above, we learn that as a rule she accompanied her parents on campaigns which must have brought her even more actively into court life. She mentions specifically having stayed with her father at Philippopolis "for some purpose or other" (XIV, 8, p. 384).

Naturally, Anna must have felt awe for her parents, which restrained her sense of freedom at court to some extent. She has told us that she was seized with wonder as she watched her mother poring over the writings of the didactic Fathers (V, 9, p. 135). On another occasion when Anna wanted to plead for the life of Anemas, the captured ringleader who had plotted to assassinate her father, she tells us that she stood fearfully outside the doors, trying to draw her mother out by signs, because her parents "were conjointly making intercessions to God" (XII, 6, p. 314). But awe for one's parents has been part of the Greek tradition from ancient times to the present. Alexios and Isaac felt the same awe for their mother. Within the framework of Byzantine family life, awe for one's parents was an ingredient of individual dignity.

Anna tells us nothing of her own immediate family at the imperial palace. As has already been stated, she speaks repeatedly of her love for her husband in the *Alexiad*, and in the Prologue to her Will she speaks of her "very handsome and fine children"; but we never see her children or learn anything about them in the history of her father.

We do get an idea of Anna's relationship to her brothers and sisters, which might have been more intimate and happier had her parents been in agreement about Alexios's successor to the throne. The Comneni family was split down the middle because of this issue concerning which each parent differed radically, even violently at times. Chalandon states that John secretly endeavored with his brother Isaac to form a party and sought to win to his cause the Senate and the people. "The task wasn't at all easy," he writes, "for John was watched closely and each of his measures was watched by his mother's spies. Despite all these obstacles the legitimate heir grouped around him a certain number of determined and energetic partisans."[1]

From what Nicetas Chionates writes, it was common knowledge that her mother never ceased trying to persuade Alexios to choose Anna and her husband to succeed him on the throne.

Nicetas paints a picture which must have occurred often to disturb the harmony of family life in the imperial family. He tells us that Irene would call John "fickle in his habits; she ridiculed his soft and luxurious life and found absolutely nothing good in his character." Alexios would listen to her exasperating importunities and try to reply with tact and diplomacy, for he liked Nicephoros Bryennios and was on good terms with his son-in-law. He may not have expected that Anna's marriage would turn out as happily as it did; nonetheless, he was pleased that it did. Anna tells us repeatedly that Irene often called on her husband, preferring him to all others for his persuasive powers and his ability to calm some bitter foe, as in the case of Bohemond. But sometimes Irene's nagging pleas were too much even for the patient and cleverly evasive Alexios; at such times, says Nicetas Chionates, he would speak to her as follows:

Madam, partner of my bed and empire, stop trying to change my mind in favor of your daughter and do not undermine the existing harmony and order, as if you were mad! Let us rather consider the question together. Who among us of all the former Emperors of the Romans (Byzantines) who had a son capable of ruling ignored him and preferred a son-in-law? Even if something like this has occurred we should not, madam, make a rule of the exception. In any case, the whole Roman Empire would laugh at me uproariously and think that I had lost my mind if I, who came to power not by lawful means but by shedding the blood of my relatives, and by methods contrary to Christian morality, when the time came to designate my successor should cast aside my flesh and blood and bring this Macedonian to my house.[2]

Bryennios was a native of Oresteias, one of the most prosperous and powerful cities in Macedonia.

This division in the Comneni household broke the tradition of unity in the imperial family established by Anna Dalassena. From what Nicetas Chionates writes, we know that Isaac was on John's side and helped him "more than anyone else to ascend the throne." Isaac, who became second Sebastocrator, was "an equal partner of his throne and table."[3] Had it not been for this division of forces within the family, Anna might have had a fine relationship with Isaac, who had gained some repute as a writer. Isaac is credited with two short works on the history of the transformation of the Homeric epic in the Middle Ages, as well as the introduction to the so-called Constantinopolitan Code of

the Octateuch in the Library of Seraglio.[4] Theodore Prodromos
wrote a discourse in which he praised Isaac for his excellence in
war, poetry, philosophy, and his love of books.[5] In his *Typikon*
of the Kosmosoteira monastery, which Isaac founded, he mentions a book which he had written in "verses, heroic, iambic and
political (popular)," also letters and descriptions. Two specimens
of his verse have been preserved, one headed *Peri Pronoias
Aporimaton*, the other a lament of forty-one lines written in
exile. He is also credited with three prose essays on Homer and
a paraphrase of Aristeias.[6]

Andronicos, Anna's younger brother, who was killed in the
war against the Turks in 1129 during the reign of John II, was
on his sister's side. She must have loved him dearly, for she
mourns him with genuine sorrow ,as she writes of him as "the
brother I held dearest" and laments his death when "he had just
reached the most charming period of his life" (XV, 5, p. 403).

From Anna's description of Maria, whom she refers to as
"my dearest sister," it would appear that this sister was also on
Anna's side. Maria was married to Nicephoros, son of Constantine
Euphorbenos Catacalon, whom Alexios had honored with the
dignity of Sebastocrator (X, 3, p. 242). From the indifferent
mention of Eudocia, her third sister may either have sided
with John or stayed out of the family quarrel completely; she
had her own sorrow to contend with. Eudocia had been married to
Iasitas Constantinios who, from what Zonaras tells us, had treated
his wife not as the daughter of a king; he had behaved toward
her as a superior, and he quarreled often with his mother-in-law.
Eudocia fell sick, and he forced her to retire to a convent.[7]
Eudocia is credited with having written a poem which has been
preserved.[8] As for her sister Theodora, married to Constantine,
Zonaras informs us that her husband was statuesque in shape and
form, but he came from a family "not of noble birth."[9] Anna
says nothing about her, possibly because Theodora's husband
was not of the nobility; despite Anna's dedication to learning
and her recognition of achievement, she was haughty about noble
birth.

We learn something of Anna's relationship to her sisters from
the way she writes about their husbands. Nicephoros Catacalon,
married to her sister Maria, receives high praise. "He knew how
to brandish a spear and cover himself with a shield," she
writes. "He was a marvel on horseback and a magnificent work of

nature; he was strong in his piety to God and sweet and gracious to men" (X, 3, p. 242). We learn nothing from Anna about her brother's wives. About John's personal life we learn only that while her father was journeying to Thessalonica, "the first son of the prince John Porphyrogenitos was born at Balabista and a little girl was born at the same time" (XII, 4, p. 309).

Anna must have gotten along well with her husband's family. She writes favorably of Marianos Mavrocatacalon, married to one of her husband's sisters; he was "truly a very brave warrior..., a braver scion of very brave ancestors" (X, 3, p. 242). She also makes laudatory remarks about her husband's grandfather, the rebel Bryennios, whom her father captured. "Bryennios," she writes, "was a very clever warrior, as well as of most illustrious descent, conspicuous by height of stature, and beauty of face, and preeminent among his fellows by the weightiness of his judgment, and the strength of his arms" (I, 4, p. 13). Her husband's family naturally sided with Anna in her aspirations for the throne; they would have been delighted to see Nicephoros sharing the throne with Anna.

It would appear that Anna's relationship to those members of her family about whom she says little, or fails to mention, must have been distant, or they may have been on John's side. She seems to have been close to her paternal and maternal uncles, especially her uncle George Palaeologos, married to her mother's sister Anna. She admittedly learned many of the facts of her history from Palaeologos. But most of her accounts she heard from her father. What becomes evident is that Anna sought involvement in the affairs of state, not only because she was devoted to her parents and was equipped to help them, but also because she herself never completely lost hope during her father's lifetime that she might succeed him on the throne.

II *Last Illness of Alexios*

For I was there myself by order of my mistress to adjudge the physicians' arguments, and I heard all they said. (XV, 11, p. 420)

The person who stands out most sharply in Anna's poignant account of her father's last illness is Anna herself, spending sleepless nights, standing watch over Alexios. It is the most three-dimensional portrait we have of her in a family group as she takes charge of things around her father's deathbed, arguing with the doctors about their different diagnoses and the varying treatments they suggested, her mother's oracular reliance on her knowledge of medicine, trying in her own way to alleviate the pain of the emperor, who was to Anna "the whole sun" and "the great lighthouse" which illuminated the world.

It is as if Anna had a doctor's chart before her at the moment of her writing, so empathic is her report of her father's condition. As she reports it, Alexios had been suffering from the wracking pains of gout for some time. Matters became very serious in the spring of 1118, when at a race track the emperor caught a bad cold, which developed into a rheumatic pain in his shoulder. At first his family saw no danger in this, but as the rheumatic attack spread to other parts of his body, they naturally became fearful, although, Anna observes, the majority of the physicians did not appreciate the danger that this threatened (XV, 11, p. 420). However, Alexios managed to recover from this attack. After a period of six months, "a deadly sickness took hold of him, caused probably by his deep despondency over daily business and the mass of public duties" (XV, 11, p. 420). The doctors could not diagnose the case, though they found "multifold irregularities" in every movement of the arteries. The most celebrated doctors of Constantinople were summoned; there was Nicolas, Callicles, poet and doctor; a friend of the Sebastos George Palaeologos; the eunuch Michael; and Michael Pantechnes, a friend of Theophylactos. All discussed her father's illness with Anna, unable to agree on the nature of the "humors" which, according to them, were the cause of the affliction which had struck the emperor. The condition of Alexios grew easier after an antidote of pepper, which gave the family new hope for his recovery, but this lasted only three or four days; his fits of suffocation attacked the lungs again; still the doctors could find no remedy for the disease, though they tried many things. They even moved the emperor from the large palace to the bright halls of Mangana Palace, where he could be more comfortable, but this did not help either. The picture that Anna paints of her mother during her father's last illness is that of a loving, grief-stricken wife,

spending a sleepless night with the Emperor, sitting behind him on the bed and supporting him in her arms and relieving his breathing somewhat . . . nursing him and continually changing his position, and devising all kinds of changes in the bedding. (XV, 11, p. 422)

We learn something more of Irene's bountiful nature when Anna tells us that her mother invoked the mercy of God upon the ailing Alexios and made numerous donations to the poor and sick:

When the Empress saw that the disease was gaining ground and she quite despaired of any human help, she made still more fervent intercessions to God on his behalf . . . and all those who were sick or confined in prison and worn out with suffering she made very rich by donations and invited them to offer prayers for the Emperor. (XV, 11, pp. 422-23)

Her sister Mary was there too, trying to ease her father's pain, giving him water to drink from a big goblet, so that drinking might not be too difficult for his inflamed palate; her sister Eudocia was also there, but all we learn about her is that "this was the third one, the Porphyrogenete" and that Eudocia had recently lost her husband and her garments were suitable for a funeral, which she could lend her mother after the death of Alexios.

What is most impressive in Anna's account is her knowledge of medicine and the authority she maintained, not only over her mother and sisters, but even over the doctors. She watched the movements of his pulse and studied his respiration (XV, 11, 3, p. 424). She describes the consultations of the doctors, their differences of opinion, the one advocating purgatives, the other forbidding them. About her own efforts she writes simply, "and yet God knows, I occupied myself diligently with the preparation of his food and brought it to him daily with my own hands and tried to make it all easy to swallow" (XV, 11, p. 423).

When they became aware that the final hour had come for Alexios and no one knew which way to turn, it was Anna to whom her mother often looked steadfastly, waiting for her "oracular decision as she had been wont to do at other critical moments," waiting for Anna's prophecy, making signs to tell her the state of her father's weakening pulse (XV, 11, p. 426). When Anna recognized that the pulse of the emperor had stopped, she tells us that she bowed her head and, exhausted and fainting, looked down to the ground and said nothing but clasped her hands over her face and stepped back and wept. The empress, who understood what that meant, "took off her royal veil and caught hold of a knife and cut off all her hair close to the skin

and threw off the red shoes from her feet and demanded ordinary
black sandals" (XV, 11, p. 426).

The only incident about her brother John that Anna adds to
this scene is "Now the Emperor's successor had already gone away
secretly to the house set apart for him, seeing the Emperor's . . .
and hastened his going and hurried to the great palace!" (XV,
11, p. 425). This is all we learn about John during the last
illness of Alexios. Anna makes no mention of her brother Isaac
or Andronicos by name, nor any other male relatives who must
surely have surrounded her father's deathbed. Had she done
so she might have unwittingly revealed a little more of what
actually happened during those last hours of her father's life.

Chalandon writes that Anna's account of what happened is
inexact. Irene and Anna took a prominent part in the events
which preceded and followed the death of Alexios. As he states,
it is precisely their attitude which obliged John to take over the
palace; it was proof that the legitimate heir had to preserve the
crown which the ambitious envy of his sister sought to capture
from him.[10]

Here is what Nicetas Chionates writes of these last hours in
the life of Alexios:

His son John, seeing his father near death, and knowing that his
mother did not love him and that she wished to bestow the kingship
on his sister, took into his confidence those of his relatives who were
friendly to him and told them of his plans. The most reliable of
these relatives was his brother Isaac. Unnoticed by his mother, John
entered his father's bedroom, fell down beside him, as if about to
break into tears, and stealthily removed the signet ring from his
finger. There are some who say that he did this with the full knowledge of his father.[11]

If we accept what Nicetas writes, then Anna and Empress
Irene must surely have seen this; shocked, they must have tried
to do something about it while the Emperor was still alive,
make every effort to have him pronounce some last-minute
decision. Nicetas reports further that when Empress Irene saw
that matters were not proceeding according to her expectation,

She went to her husband who was lying on his bed, showing only
weak signs of life, and throwing herself upon his body, began to
inveigh loudly against her son "shedding tears like a black fountain"
calling him a thief and accusing him of having designs on the throne,

while his father was still alive, and of planning a rebellion. But her husband did not answer her, being naturally concerned with the more serious questions of how long he had to live, reflecting on his departure from this life which was not very far off, and directing his eyes toward the angels who receive and guide the souls. As the empress, unable to bear the conduct of her son, kept pressing her husband, Alexios, with a slight forced smile lifted his hands toward heaven. Perhaps he was pleased at her report and thanking God for what had happened; or, as he glanced at his wife with a smile, he may have been about to make a taunting remark to the one who had the heart to speak of the succession at a time when his soul was about to leave his body; or, he may have been begging God's forgiveness for having wandered from the path of righteousness. The woman doubtless thought her husband was pleased with what she had told him. She felt entirely cheated of her previous hopes and utterly disappointed of all promises. With a deep groan she said "My husband, throughout your active life, you surpassed all men in every sort of wiliness; you were always a master of doubletalk and even now, as you are about to quit life, you have not changed at all."

"This then," says Nicetas, "is what happened there."[12]

As can be seen, this dramatic account by the Byzantine historian is radically different from Anna's recollection of the last hours in her father's life and John's accession. Zonaras also believes that Alexios died with a smile on his lips and that John took the signet ring off the hand of his father with the approval of the dying man.[13]

The mortal remains of Alexios were carried the next morning in a solemn procession to the Christ Philanthropos monastery which he had founded. John did not go to the funeral, but clung to the royal palace "as polyps do to rocks."[14] He had to be prudent about running the risk of a confrontation with those who coveted the throne, but he did send most of his relatives to his father's funeral.

Alexios died on August 15, 1118. He had reigned over the Byzantine Empire for thirty-seven years, four months, and fifteen days. John II was thirty years old when he ascended the throne. Anna was thirty-five. At his accession, John II Comnenos placed Irene and Anna in the convent of Kecharitomene.

III   *Anna's Plot to Assassinate John II (1118-1143)*

He was the best type of all the Emperors from the family of the Comneni who had ever sat upon the Roman throne. (Nicetas

Chionates, *Historia* ed. I Bekker, *Corpus Scriptorum Historiae Byzantinae*, pp. 64-65)

The *Alexiad* offers no information about what took place after
John hastened out of the Palace Mangana where his father lay
dying, with Alexios's signet ring securely placed on his own
finger. Again the reader must turn to other Byzantine historians if
he wishes to learn what happened directly after the death of
Alexios. As Nicetas Chionates and other Byzantine historians recount these events, John with his troops, his brother Isaac, and
other relatives who favored his accession proceeded to the great
palace. At the same time, he sent word to the patriarch
announcing the death of Alexios and asked to be crowned immediately. From what they write, he seems to have found no
obstacle there. John gained entrance to the great palace but not
before a struggle with the Varangian Guard, which forced his
followers to lift the doors off the hinges. Alexios died during the
night, but John did not budge from the great palace once he
gained entrance. He even disregarded his mother's invitation to
attend his father's funeral, "not because he was unwilling to do
honor to his father," writes Nicetas, "but because he was afraid
of his rivals who were still coveting his throne."[15] The family was
openly divided now. His sister Anna, his mother, Bryennios, and
his brother Andronicos were on one side; John, Isaac, and his followers were on the other. John waited to see who would make
the next move.

Nothing happened directly after Alexios was laid to rest,
although the quiet which followed was the calm before the
storm. John started his rule a few days later, following in his
father's footsteps, and honoring with titles and dignities all those
who had supported his ascension to the throne. His brother
Isaac became Sebastocrator, which made him "an equal partner
of his throne and his table."[16] It was the way his uncle
Isaac had been honored during his father's reign. All seemed
to be going forward as John had hoped.

But the other side had not ceased in its plans to overthrow
John. Less than a year after John's reign had begun, Anna headed
a conspiracy to assassinate her brother and place her husband on
the throne. The conspirators chose to execute their *coup de grâce*
when John II was spending the night at the Hippodrome of
the Philopation, one of the imperial residences outside the capital

near the Golden Gate, where the conspirators had succeeded in
bribing the guards. Bryennios was to give the signal for the
conspirators to storm the residence and assassinate John.

But Nicephoros Bryennios, the man whom Anna admired for
his literary pursuits and his love of books, was evidently less
greedy for power and did not wish to carry out his wife's planned
conspiracy against her brother. Curiously enough, neither his wife
nor their conspirators detected Bryennios's true feelings about
the matter; his quiet resolve not to execute his wife's violent plan
he kept to himself until after the conspirators were caught and
the whole plot was disclosed to Emperor John II. Nicetas writes
that the plot failed "because of the dull and sluggish Bryennios
who was in the country and forgot his arrangements with the conspirators."[17] It hardly seems possible that Nicephoros would
have forgotten so important an assignment. Enraged at her husband's failure to appear at the post which would have given the
conspirators the signal agreed on, Anna lashed out at her husband
and at nature for having made her a woman and her husband
a man.

When the plot was discovered, the property of all the conspirators was confiscated, though most of it was later restored.
Anna's property went to John's Grand Domestic John Axuchos,
a Persian by nationality and a child prisoner whom Alexios had
captured during the siege of Nicaea and raised with his son John.
Axuchos, an able administrator in the reign of John II, was also
interested in Christian metaphysics and was in close touch with
contemporary scholars and theologians. Axuchos refused Anna's
property and urged John to return it to her; although he admitted
that Anna was guilty, he said that she was still the sister "of a
good ruler who would regain once more by her repentance and
with the help of nature, the love which she had lost through her
folly."[18]

Anna's career at the Byzantine court ended with her father's
death. From her complete silence on the events which took place
during her brother's and her nephew Manuel's reign, which followed that of John II, it would appear that she no longer mixed
in political or military events or any other public happenings
at the imperial court. After the accession of John II she lived most
often at the convent Kecharitomene. It was at this convent that
she wrote her *Alexiad* which starts at 1069 and ends with her
father's death.

IV   *Anna and Her Family During the Reign of John II*

But all that was most desirable vanished together with the Emperor, and his efforts were all rendered vain after his departure by the stupidity of his successors to the throne. (XIV, 3, 3, p. 371)

The return of her confiscated property did not lessen Anna's hatred of her brother John. From the above statement, it can be seen that Anna did not think much of her brother's rule. So far as she was concerned, her father who was "more solicitous of the universal welfare than his own," had failed in his objective. "For after him," she writes, "things were different and everything was turned into confusion" (XIV, 3, 3, pp. 370-71).

Despite what Anna writes, contemporary historians regard John II as one of the greatest Byzantine emperors. Both Greek and Latin chroniclers agree that John, who earned the surname of Caloyan (John the Good) merited the general respect of the populace because of his high moral qualities. Nicetas Chionates wrote that everyone praised John "as the finest of all the Romans who sat on the throne."[19] John lowered taxation and abolished capital punishment, which was unprecedented; he never mutilated anyone guilty of a crime.[20] In 1123 the Patzinaks, who had remained quiet ever since their defeat in 1091 at Lebunium, crossed the Danube and spread over the country north of Mount Haemus. John annihilated them completely. In memory of this victory John set up a trophy and even instituted a special "Patzinak celebration" which, according to Nicetas Chionates, "was still celebrated to that day in commemoration of the victory and in gratitude to God."[21] Ostrogorsky reports that in view of the danger of Norman power in south Italy, John II formed an entente first with Lothair of Germany; then, after the latter's death, with Conrad III. Pisa was also drawn into this anti-Norman alliance, and in 1136, John confirmed the trading privileges which his father once granted it.[22] John II reigned successfully for a quarter of a century until his death of a poisoned wound in 1143. During his reign, Byzantium regained most of its former boundaries. Cilicia was conquered; Byzantium was enlarged by the annexation of Armenia Minor, and after a short siege, reached the borders of Antioch, which surrendered to John.[23] John II founded the monastery of Pantocrator in 1136, with many charitable institutions; he instituted a hospital in it with fifty beds, a consultation room with a pharmacy annexed to it, an almshouse for twenty-four old men, well equipped with nurses and surgeons. It had three churches.[24] When John II died, his heir found an even stronger empire than John received at the death of his father.

Anna's brief listing of the campaigns fought by her brother John reveals nothing of the significance of these campaigns for Byzantium; actually, they were outstanding victories for John II. It is John and not his father whom historians credit for the complete annihilation of the Patzinaks in 1123, although his father did win a tremendous victory against the Patzinaks in 1091 at Lebunium.

Anna mentions John three times to state three facts about him: his birth and the twins born to John and his wife Princess Prisca in 1104; and she includes John's name officially in the treaty between Alexios and Bohemond, which ended the last struggle between them in which the Norman repeated his pledges of faith to Alexios and his "thrice-longed for son, the Emperor and Lord John Porphyrogenitos." She could not very well omit John's right to succession from the official document which she quotes verbatim and in its entirety.

From what we learn of John's forgiving nature, he may even have attempted a reconciliation with his sister. We know that Andronicos, who had openly sided with Anna, repented. John, who believed that "a strong thing is affection interwoven with kinship," forgave him, and Andronicos again lived at the court with his brother, continuing to serve John until his death in 1129. Nicephoros Bryennios also lived at the palace, and, as Anna herself states in her Preface, her husband accompanied his brother-in-law on several of his campaigns and held high office in his administration. John gladly forgave Isaac after he tried to stir up foreign enemies against him. John's home life was conducive to friendship; he and his wife had eight children, four daughters and four sons, whom John took with him on several of his campaigns. Princess Prisca, who had changed her name to Irene when John ascended the throne, was praised for her modesty and charity. Both she and her husband constructed the monastery of Pantocrator. Irene died on August 13, 1134 in Bithynia; on her deathbed she took the monastic habit and the name of Xene.[25]

Anna's two sons and two daughters were treated kindly by their uncle. John II had Prodromos compose the already mentioned *Epithalamium* extolling the virtues of his nephew Alexios,

who had married the daughter of the king of Georgia, David II,
and of John, who married Theodora.[26] Both marriages were celebrated by their uncle with nuptial festivities. But so far as is
known, John and Anna were never reconciled.

V Death of Nicephoros Bryennios; Anna's Retreat to Convent Kecharitomene; the Writing of the Alexiad

He returned to the Queen of Cities suffering from an internal tumor
caused by his incessant sufferings. (Preface, 3, p. 3)

The only cloud in Anna's otherwise happy marriage was her
husband's inability to fulfill her conspiratorial plans to overthrow
her brother John, although this disappointment appears nowhere
in the Alexiad. She is full of praise for her husband; she writes
proudly of his military successes during her father's reign, which
he continued in the reign of her brother John, although Anna
has no heart to give us any more than a listing of the campaigns
which ended his life so unexpectedly. She offers no historical
or military analysis of these campaigns.

Anna was totally indifferent to the reigns of her brother and
her nephew Manuel, though she survived her brother by a number
of years and lived several years after her nephew's succession to
the throne. But even in her cursory listing of her husband's last
campaigns, we get a picture of Nicephoros Bryennios as a responsible man, who thought little of his own welfare.

In reliving the last days of her husband's life, when he returned
home seriously ill from one of the campaigns with her brother
John, Anna acquaints us with the probable causes of his illness,
the endless discomfort of a soldier's life, his many expeditions,
or again his overwhelming anxiety over her and their children.
Her soul is torn to pieces, and even the memory of their last
scene together overwhelms her soul with dizziness and tears
blind her eyes; she wonders how she has been able to survive
so much (Preface, 4, p. 4).

When Bryennios returned to the capital so gravely ill, Anna
must have nursed him with the same devotion and skill that she
displayed during her father's last illness, although she says nothing
of that. She tells us only that her husband was anxious to tell the
tragic story of his adventure. She forbade it not only because he
was unable to do so because of his disease but because she feared
that the effort might cause the tumor to burst. Once again, we

have another instance of her knowledge of medicine. Nicephoros died in 1138, when he was fifty-seven years old.

VI *Anna's Last Years*

We clearly owe much to the drive and inspiration of this astonishing lady whose memory is enshrined not only in the immortal history of her father's reign, but also in the austere volume of the *Commentaria Graeca in Aristotelem.* (Robert Browning, "An Unpublished Funeral Oration of Anna Comnena," by Georgios Tornikes, p. 10)

From what Tornikes says of Anna, whom he refers to constantly as "basilissa," her greatest intellectual fulfillment and her contribution to letters came after the death of her father and more particularly during the years of her enforced retirement from public life. From this account, it was certainly not as pathetic as Anna makes it sound. The convent Kecharitomene, overlooking the Golden Horn, gave our historian the serenity she probably never enjoyed in the imperial palace. Although she did not reside there permanently until the death of her husband, it was there that she made her greatest contribution, not only as a historian, but as an educator and as a woman of letters. It was at the convent Kecharitomene that Anna intensified her intellectual pursuits. Tornikes tells us that Anna gathered about her a philosophic circle whose work she inspired and directed.[27] In particular we learn that she encouraged Aristotelian commentators; Tornikes mentions the name of Michael of Ephesus whom he himself had heard speak of the basilissa as the cause of damage to his eyes, because he had to work nights without sleep on the commentaries of the works of Aristotle which Anna supervised.[28] Michael of Ephesus wrote commentaries on zoological and anthropological works and on the *Rhetoric* and the *Politics.*

Anna and her daughter Irene must surely have enjoyed the privileges at the convent Kecharitomene set in her mother's *Typikon* for imperial princesses and nuns. Yet from the way Anna writes, she felt like an outsider, despite the dignity and ease of her surroundings and despite the scholarly group who revered her. "For the powers that be have condemned us to this ridiculous position so that we should not be seen, but be a general object of abhorrence" (XIV, 7, 3, p. 382). Anna felt the greatest sense of belonging in her father's imperial court, participating in the comings and goings in the palace, basking in the adoration of her parents, especially of her mother, admired by the aristocracy who looked upon her as the most scintillating woman of the Byzantine nobility. Tornikes states that Anna took the veil at her deathbed. Both Browning and Darrouzès are inclined to date Anna's death to the years 1153-55, from the probable date of the delivery of Tornikes's funeral oration.

CHAPTER 5

Alexios Comnenos, Byzantine Military Strategist

I Service of Alexios (1056-1081)

ALEXIOS fought in three campaigns against rebels during the reigns of two different Emperors before his own accession. In these campaigns against Ursel, Nicephoros Bryennios, and Basilacios, Alexios appears in Anna's history largely as a political strategist who captures each of his adversaries through military strategy and diplomacy.

His first military assignment came when Michael VII Ducas sent him to capture the rebel Ursel, a Frank by birth, who had enrolled in the Roman army and had laid waste nearly all the eastern provinces. At this time Alexios served as lieutenant under his elder brother Isaac, who was commander-in-chief of all the Armies of the East and West (I, 1, p. 8). As usual, Anna highlights her father's valor, as well as his victory, by telling us that many men of high reputation for bravery, knowledge of war, and long experience in fighting, had been sent after Ursel, but they could not capture the rebel because he made "meteor-like attacks," was "irresistible in his onrushes," "utterly confounded their phalanxes," while her father captured Ursel "within the space of a few days." For this victory, Emperor Michael appointed Alexios Absolute Commander, although he still had "the first down on his cheeks" (I, 1, p. 8).

What Anna admires most about her father is that he knew how to offer the hand of friendship with words, gifts, and large sums of money to an ally of the enemy he was sent to capture, thus making it possible for him to conquer both in the end. In the case of Ursel, the rebel had formed an alliance with the Turk Tutach, who was ravaging Roman territory on the east. Alexios, blessed with the power of persuasion, succeeded in separating Ursel from his ally by convincing Tutach and his followers that

101

Ursel was lifting his hand against the sultan as well as the
emperor. With promises of money, the goodwill of the emperor,
and hostages, he persuaded Tutach and his followers to seize
Ursel, whom they turned over to Alexios at Amasia. When the
promised money did not come, Tutach and his followers demanded the return of Ursel and threatened rebellion. Using
great ingenuity, Alexios decided to borrow the money from the
inhabitants of Amasia. After calming down the rebels, Alexios
pretended to have Ursel blinded, "while the victim groaned like
a lion roaring," in order to appease Tutach and his followers for
capturing Ursel. "This bit of playacting," Anna writes, "persuaded
the whole multitude, natives and foreigners alike, to swarm in
like bees to pay their contributions" (1, 3, p. 11). The whole point
of Alexios's device was to foil the possible plans of the rebels to
rescue Ursel. Alexios continued to serve Michael VII by annexing
several more cities and fortresses, Anna writes, and placed under
the protection of the emperor those who had suffered during
Ursel's regime (I, 3, p. 12).

After the overthrow of Michael VII, Emperor Botaneiates appointed Alexios Domestic of the Schools.[1] He also honored him
with the rank of Proedros in charge of the defense of Constantinople and sent him to war against the rebel General Nicephoros
Bryennios, Duke of Dyrrachium: "a very clever warrior" who
headed the right and left wings of a huge army. Anna writes
of his enormous army and the bravery of Bryennios, "circling
like an Ares or Giant and an object of dread to onlookers,"
probably to focus more sharply her father's dauntlessness when
he had only a very few "Immortals," a few soldiers from Coma,
and a Celtic regiment of only a few men (I, 5, p. 15). Anna's
vividly colorful and exciting description of this battle array
highlights the bravery and confidence of Alexios as he marshalled
his meager forces against a powerful foe. Again, Anna presents
her father mainly as a strategist, examining the topography,
dividing his men into two sections, one of which was hidden,
and arousing their bravery with "winged words." When the
Scythians on Bryennios's side routed Alexios's men, no small
confusion arose in the ranks as the standards of both sides
commingled. Alexios, who was cut off, moved about within the
army of the enemy, seized Bryennios's horse, which was decked
with a purple cloth and gilt bosses, and escaped unnoticed by
the men in Bryennios's army. When he arrived in a safe spot,

Alexios, who held Bryennios's horse, commanded a herald to shout out that Bryennios had fallen. This brought back to battle all of Alexios's scattered soldiers and encouraged them to carry on (I, 5, pp. 16, 17).

Things might not have ended victoriously for Alexios, despite his strategy and his valor, were it not for the timely arrival of a detachment of Turkish allies who joined Alexios at a moment when the lines were all mixed up and Alexios's contingent of Franks had gone over to Bryennios in the midst of the battle. Again Alexios relied on strategy to lure the enemy, dividing his forces into three parts, two of which remained in ambush, showering arrows upon them from all sides, until Bryennios's army retreated. Soldiers seized the rebel and brought him to Alexios, who sent him to Emperor Botaneiates without doing any injury to his eyes. "If later on undesirable things happened to Bryennios," writes Anna, "the blame must be laid on certain of the Emperor's courtiers; my father was blameless" (I, 6, 5, p. 20). According to Anna's husband, it was Borilos who blinded Bryennios.[2]

Emperor Botaneiates next sent Alexios to Thessaly to crush the usurper Basilacios, another rebel who had designs on the throne. Anna again gives us an epic description of this rebel as "one of the most conspicuous for bravery, courage, daring and bodily strength." A little later she adds, "besides other admirable qualities, this man had that fine physique, strength of arm, and dignified appearance by which rustics are most attracted" (I, 7, 1, pp. 20-21).

Basilacios had under his command the whole army of Illyria and Bulgaria, as well as the Varangians which Emperor Michael had sent to Basilacios.[3] Undaunted, Alexios sized up the topography of the place, then pitched his camp on a piece of dry ground with the running river on one side as a bulwark, and he used the old river bed which had become a ravine as a natural trench. This time, Alexios cunningly planned another device to deceive the enemy. He had camp fires burning on all sides and his own tent illuminated with lamps, expecting that Basilacios would attack his tent first, while "he himself drew off to a good distance with his troops" (I, 7, 4, p. 22).

Things happened as Alexios had planned. Basilacios rushed first into the gleaming tent. "Little John," the monk Alexios always had with him to please his mother, had been deliberately

left behind to trick Basilacios. When Basilacios did not see
Alexios, he cried out wild with fury, "Where in the world is the
Stammerer?" This gives Anna the opportunity to explain to us
that her father was a natural orator, but his tongue lisped slightly
on the letter "r" (I, 8, pp. 22-23). At that moment, Anna tells us,
Alexios loomed before them and began a wild attack on them.
Alexios "used the place, the time, everything as a means to
victory," writes his daughter, "and availed himself of them with
unperturbed and unshaken judgement" (I, 8, p. 23). An added
suspenseful bit is the story about Alexios emerging from the
enemy camp and almost being cut down by one of his own men.
Alexios pursued the fleeing Basilacios to Thessalonika where
the rebel was received. The gates, however, were barred before
Alexios, who then encamped there and threatened to besiege and
sack the city unless they surrendered Basilacios. Finally, the
Thessalonians, fearing that their city would be destroyed, allowed Alexios to enter. The inhabitants and custodians of the
Acropolis, where Basilacios had taken refuge, drove the rebel
out against his will and handed him over to the emperor. Alexios,
who immediately sent news of his capture to his emperor, stayed
a little longer in Thessalonika, "to arrange things there" (I, 9,
p. 25). Anna's husband explains that Alexios found immense
treasures in Thessalonika, which he seized. He remained in the
city a number of days, established order, and returned to Constantinople with glorious trophies.[4] As a reward for her father's
successes and achievements, the emperor raised him to the rank
of "Sebastos" and proclaimed him Sebastos in public assembly.
These three campaigns, which Anna calls "Labors" were accom-
plished by her father, "a second Hercules," before he himself
revolted and ascended the Byzantine throne.

II   His Ascension to the Throne

On the Saturday named after cheese, bravo to you for your shrewdness, Alexius! But on the Monday after the Sunday you flew away like
a high-flying hawk out of the nests of the barbarians. (II, 4, p. 52)

Probably the most picturesque and dramatic section in Anna's
history is her account of her father's lightning revolt which elevated him to the Byzantine throne. The immediate occasion for the
revolt was the city of Cyzicus, which the Turks had seized and
which Alexios was called on to defend. On the night of Quinqua-

gesima Sunday, which Anna identifies as Cheese-eating Sunday,[5] Alexios and his brother Isaac made their arrangements to revolt. The following day at dawn they had already left the city with their partisans. The populace, who approved of her father's spirit, wove the little song quoted above in their own popular dialect to cheer him on to success (II, 4, 2, p. 52). It is interesting to note that this is one of the very few instances where Anna recognizes the spoken language of the people.

Anna's account of the revolt of the Comneni tells the dramatic story of the Comneni and the Ducas families who united to place Alexios on the throne. What sparked the revolt was the plan of Borilos and Germanos, the two Scythian favorites of Botaneiates, to get the Comneni out of the way by blinding them. The brothers learned about this from a certain Alanian; it was then that the Comneni decided that their only hope of safety lay in open rebellion. The brothers organized their plan to line up all influential followers. George Palaeologos hesitated before giving his support to the revolt, because his father was extremely devoted to Emperor Botaneiates. However, once he decided to join Alexios, largely because of the firm injunction of his mother-in-law Maria, he gave himself entirely to the revolt (II, 6, p. 56).

One of the most dramatic episodes in the revolt involved Caesar John Ducas who was staying in his estates Ta Moroboundou in Thrace in the spring of 1081. The Comneni, who were eager to have him join in their revolt, and who were fully aware of his idiosyncrasies, sent him a message which, Anna notes, "had an excellent touch of wit." "We on our side," it said, "have prepared a right good meal, not wanting in rich condiments, but if you on your side wish to share this banquet, you must come with all speed to partake of it." The caesar "grasped his beard for a time," then yielded to their wish and rode off to join the rebellion (II, 6, p. 57). The whole world was agog with excitement, Anna tells us, as the gathering crowds headed toward the capital. She justifies her father's shrewdness for suborning the guards of the walls to capture the city (II, 9, p. 63).

Probably Alexios's most judicious act to secure his kingship was to elevate his brother-in-law, Nicephoros Melissenos, who also aspired to the throne, to the rank of "Caesar" with all the privileges of that rank, and also to give him the largest town in Thessaly, which Alexios signed in a Golden Bull (II, 8, p. 62).

When the Comneni had taken possession of the palace, Alexios went to live in the "Upper" palace (also named Boucoleon) with his brothers, mother, and nearest male relations; he left his fifteen-year-old wife with her sisters and her paternal grand-father in the "Lower" palace. Patriarch Cosmas crowned Alexios alone. "When," Anna informs us, "the imperial diadem had not yet been conferred on the Queen," the Ducas family was alarmed and insisted on Queen Irene's coronation (III, 2, p. 75). George Palaeologos, who had won the fleet over to the side of the Com-neni, sailed to the Acropolis with the men cheering for Alexios. When he arrived in Constantinople and they started the acclama-tions, he defied the warning not to join the name of Irene to that of Alexios by shouting up to those who warned him, "It is not for you that I undertook this heavy conflict, but just her you men-tion, Irene." "And straightway," Anna concludes, "he bade the sailors shout for Irene, as well as Alexios" (III, 2, p. 73).

According to Anna, Patriarch Cosmas crowned Alexios without the queen because the newly acclaimed emperor was compelled to plunge into military matters as soon as he ascended the throne. As has already been stated, Anna Dalassena tried to prevent Irene's coronation and connived to get Patriarch Cosmas, a friend of the Ducas family, to resign. Cosmas agreed to do this only after he had crowned Irene. This he succeeded in doing, in Hagia Sophia,[6] seven days after he had crowned Alexios emperor in the same church.

CHAPTER 6

The Reign of Alexios I (1081-1118)

I The Role of Alexios in Domestic Affairs

... who possessed neither forces nor money and had only just taken over a state already corrupt which had for a long time been gradually diminishing and had sunk practically to the lowest depths. (*Alexiad*, III, 11, p. 95)

ANNA was not exaggerating when she wrote of the corrupt state her father inherited when he ascended the throne. It was true that "the Roman Empire possessed only a very insufficient army ... there was no large reserve of money in the imperial treasury with which to hire allied troops from foreign countries" (III, 9, p. 90). Enemies surrounded Alexios on all sides. "At home," Anna writes, "disaffection was rife, and abroad rebellions never ceased" (XII, 5, p. 310). In 1081, the year that Alexios became emperor, Anna relates that Robert Guiscard took possession of Corfu and began to attack the mainland. He had already taken Valona with forces he had brought with him and innumerable troops were rallying to his standard from all quarters. He had penetrated inland as far as Macedonia and Thessaly. In Asia, the Turks were already in possession of Cappadocia, Iconium, Philadelphia, Smyrna, Sebastea, and New Caesarea. Now they were harassing the frontiers. There were dangerous insurrections in Cyprus and Crete; Alexios had to send a large fleet and a garrison to Crete and Cyprus to guard both of these islands by land and by sea (IX, 2, p. 219). Truly, Alexios had his back against the wall.

Alexios was forced to take extreme measures to raise the money needed to free the Byzantine Empire of the dangers which threatened its very survival. From what Anna has told us, at first her father appealed to his family and persons well disposed toward the imperial family who voluntarily offered to help him. Empress Irene gave her husband all her jewelry so he might

107

raise an army against Robert Guiscard. From other relatives and
friends he received silver and gold articles and sent them to the
imperial mint. But this was hardly enough. He needed much
more money to pay soldiers who asked for rewards, "on the plea
that they had fought on the Emperor's side, and others who were
mercenaries kept clamoring for higher pay" (V, 2, p. 117). He
needed money to ransom prisoners of war, furnish pay for allies,
pay for troops; he had to raise, collect, and train an army thoroughly and weld them into one, all of which required money.
He had to combat the incursions of the Turks, the raids of the
Patzinaks, and the swords of the Normans (VI, 3, p. 142).

Anna mentions only two other means her father used to raise
the money so desperately needed. One of these was his appropriation of some unused church property which he turned into
coin in order to supply ships of war and cavalry, train an army,
and pay the Turks on the east, whom he had to recruit for help
to fight the Normans (V, 2, p. 117). Ostrogorsky states that he
pawned these.[1] This was an extraordinary measure for so pious
a man even to consider, much less carry out even in an emergency.
Bishop Leo, who headed the Church of Chalcedon, did everything in his power to frustrate the plans of Alexios to have the
appropriation of the church property legalized by the church.
In his defense before the Assembly, Alexios stated that he needed
the money to recall the scattered troops by offering them bribes
and to collect allies from all sides "who would easily be allured
by the promise of heavy largess" (V, 1, p. 117).

In a novel that Alexios published later, we have a record of
the emperor's humble restitution of the church property which
he had taken for military expenses and a new army, with an
edict forbidding his successors from a similar spoliation of church
property; he himself comprehended the dangerous precedent he
had set.[2] According to his daughter, he presented himself as a
defendant before a large assembly of clergy, the military, and
the Senate. After his defense he made lavish reparations to the
churches from which he had taken the treasures (VI, 3, p. 142).

His greatest need for money was to renew the war with Robert
Guiscard. In order to do this, Anna writes that her father urged
the Venetians by letter to furnish a large fleet, promising them
that they should have their expenses paid many times over, provided they would equip their whole navy and with all speed sail
to Dyrrachium to protect the city and engage in battle with

Robert's fleet (IV, 2, p. 100). To strengthen his depleted cavalry, Alexios bought thoroughbred horses from Damascus, Edessa, and Arabia. Anna points out that after a successful battle with Robert in Dyrrachium, Alexios received the Venetians "with great honor, bestowed many benefactions upon them and then dismissed them with a large gift of money for the Doge of Venice and his subordinate magistrates" (IV, 2, p. 101). Anna's list includes only a few of these honors bestowed on the Venetians which Alexios recorded in May 1082 in a Chrysobull (Novel 32). These are:

1. The doge of Venice is honored with the title of Protosebastos 'with salary attached.
2. The Patriarch receives the title Hypertimios and a corresponding salary.
3. A large yearly sum of gold is decreed to all the churches of Venice.
4. All the shopkeepers in Constantinople who are natives of Amalfi are to pay tribute to the Church in Venice named after the apostle Mark.
5. The Venetians received all the wharfs running from the old Hebraic anchorage to that called Bigla, and all the anchorages between these two, as well as much real property, not only in the capital, and in Dyrrachium, but wherever they asked for it.
6. Venetian merchandise was not to be taxed in any country under Roman sway. (VI, 5, pp. 146-47)

It is interesting to compare Anna's less complete account of the concessions to the Venetians with the chief provisions of the Alexian Chrysobull as recorded by Horatio F. Brown.[3]

1. Venice is to receive 20 pounds annually...
2. The Doge and his successors are to enjoy the title of Protosebastos with an ample revenue.
3. The Patriarch of Grado and his successors are to enjoy the title of Hypertimon with a revenue of 20 pounds.
4. The Church of San Marco in Venice is to receive from each Amalfitano trading in Constantinople and the Empire three perperi yearly.
5. A concession to the Venetians of a Quarter in Constantinople with shops in the district of the Ferry between the Gates called the Jews' Gate and the gate called the Watch Gate with all occupied and unoccupied lands, and comprising three wharfs or landing stages on the shores of the Golden Horn; also the Church of S. Akyndini with its bakery and revenue of twenty bezants.

6. A concession to the Church of S. Andrea in Durazzo with its revenue from the fisc.

7. The Venetians acquire the right to trade, free of any charge whatever, in all parts of Byzantium.

8. The Venetians are under obligation to defend the Empire.

9. Sanction for infringement of Venetian privileges is a fine of ten pounds of gold and four times the value of goods misappropriated.

Alexios's Novel 36 also makes concessions to the Pisans. The result of Venetian support was that Alexios was able to conclude a favorable peace with the Normans. But the effect on the domestic life of Byzantium was disastrous. Native merchants complained that the Venetians were enabled to undersell them in every market.[4]

The money that Alexios received from his family and from those subjects of his empire who were well disposed to him, and the church property he had appropriated, could never pay for the disastrous concessions to the Venetians listed in the Alexian Chrysobull, nor could the emperor pay for the lavish rewards he had to give his faithful followers and his family, nor to the crusaders who swarmed into Byzantine territory in 1096. How then did Alexios raise the large sums of money which he distributed so prodigally?

The only other means that Anna records is that her father confiscated the property of criminals, rebels, and those who had plotted against his life. He had to do much more than that to raise the enormous sums of money he needed. As Joan Hussey asserts, Alexios was compelled to raise money by the exaction of heavy taxes, which bore most heavily on the poorest classes, who were now liable to taxation for the first time. Their burden was made heavier by labor services, billeting, as well as the exorbitant taxes exacted by tax-farmers.[5]

One of the most significant domestic developments introduced during the reign of Alexios was the *pronoia*, granting revenue from the estate to the holder or *pronoiar* in return for military service. These conditional grants in *pronoia*, strengthened the defenses of the Byzantine Empire and the military aristocracy; it also contributed to the progress of feudalization. As Ostrogorsky explained it, "the *pronoiar* now had the obligation of military service and for this reason was generally called 'soldier' (stratiotis). He was an equipped and mounted knight and, in accordance with the value of his *pronoia* grant, he was accompanied by a varying number of troops."[6]

Alexios also handed over to laymen the administration of monasteries and monastic property. This practice, known as *charistikium,* aimed at promoting the economic development of the monastic property. It did not compel the recipient to perform military service, but it did provide the state with a source of revenue. Whoever owned the monastery gave it for life to a person who came to be known as the *charistikarios.* He "received all the revenues of the monastery and he was obliged to maintain the monks and take care of the buildings. It is evident that the surplus of the revenues belonged to the *charistikarios.*"[7]

The *pronoia* system intensified the feudalizing process which helped to spread serfdom and sustain slavery. The *charistikium* corrected some of the abuses caused by the excessive wealth of the monks, but the greater profits went to the *charistikarios* and not to the state. The *pronoia* aided Alexios in having a reserve of armed forces that he could call upon without maintaining a large, expensive standing army of professionals who might revolt over back pay promotions or who might seize power unchecked by other available forces; nor did he have to depend on unreliable mercenaries. However, both the *pronoia* and the *charistikium* ultimately diminished the government revenue and helped in its final decline.[8]

Alexios also raised money by exacting forced loans, confiscating property from magnates and the church, punishing with fines rather than imprisonments, selling privileges, farming out taxes, granting immunity to private landowners, and increasing the depreciation of the coinage. He attempted to check debasement and inflation by ruling that the *nomisma* should be stabilized at a third of its original value. Vasiliev makes clear that "along with the former golden coins of full weight, which were called *nomisma, hyperpyron,* or *solidus,* he had put into circulation a certain alloy of copper and gold or silver and gold called *nomisma.* . . . The new nomisma as compared to the former, which consisted of twelve silver coins or *miliarisia,* was equal in value only to four silver coins, one third as much."[9]

It must be said, however, that not all the money Alexios exacted from his subjects was used for military defense. These measures did fall inequitably on the masses; as for the fines he exacted from culprits, these were usually regarded as a highly desirable alternative. Alexios used some of this money to found charitable institutions, and he gave public assistance generously. He founded a community on the Golden Horn, which consisted of a number of institutions: an orphanage around the Church of Saint Paul, which Anna describes at length, consisted of a hospital, almshouse, and a school; Alexios saw to it that orphans of all races received a good general education. "It was a second city inside the Queen of Cities," writes his daughter, "And all around in a circle were a number of houses, dwellings for the poor and ...residences for mutilated men" (XV, 7, p. 409). He also used money to correct abuses in the monasteries. While he cut down the excessive wealth of some monasteries he lavished privileges on others, as on the monastery of Saint John the Baptist on the island of Patmos under Christodoulos.[10]

Alexios also used some of the money he raised for scholars in the development of literature and art. The reign of the Comneni is known as the Second Golden Age of Byzantine Art. Alexios spared no expense to encourage the taste for literature, for the classics, for the study of the Scriptures, and for education. Oman states that Alexios dragged the empire out of the deepest slough of degradation and ruin that it had ever sunk into.[11] Thanks to his vigor and prudence, the empire during his reign was extended north, south, and west to the Danube, to Cilicia and the Adriatic. Anna writes proudly that her father succeeded in enlarging the circle of his rule, for on the west he made the Adriatic Sea his frontier, and on the east the Euphrates and Tigris (VI, 11, p. 159).

II *His Struggle Against the Turks and Patzinaks*

For in the East the Turks were grievously harassing the frontiers. (III, 9, p. 89)

Alexios's struggle with the Turks occupies Anna's attention in ten of her fifteen books in the *Alexiad*. Her report on the Patzinaks is of particular importance since hers is the only account we have of this nomadic tribe.[12] She probably received her information as she did her other accounts, from old officers of her father, from Alexios himself, or from George Palaeologos, her maternal uncle.

When Alexios ascended the throne in 1081, Syria was lost to the Turks, and the Seljuk Sulayman, Sultan of Iconium, had obtained Nicaea, only seventy miles from Constantinople. We know from Anna that Sulayman was living around the Propontis, encamped around Nicaea (where he had his "*sultanicium*") and raiding the country around Bithynia and Thynia, making incursions as far as the Bosporos (III, 11, p. 93).

Alexios was engaged in a battle with the Seljuks soon after he ascended the throne. He succeeded in routing them out of the provinces of Nicomedia, but judged it expedient to accept the sultan's proposal of peace so that he could turn his attention to Robert Guiscard who was invading Dyrrachium.

When the sultan Sulayman left Nicaea, he appointed his relative Abu'l Qasim (Anna calls him Apelchasem) general-in-chief and governor of Nicaea. Under Abu'l Qasim, the Turks had penetrated as far as the Propontis and the maritime towns there. Matters grew worse for the Byzantine Empire when Philaretos, former ally of Nicephoros Botaneiates, defected to the Turks and made himself master of the province of Antioch. In the meantime, Sulayman took Iconium (Konya) and in 1084 occupied Cilicia. Sulayman received an appeal from one of the native factions hostile to Philaretos, entered Antioch, took it without a blow, and transferred Cappadocia to his brother Pulchases. Claude Cahen believes that Sulayman succeeded because of a measure of authorization from Alexios himself.[13]

Abu'l Qasim established himself on the shores of the Aegean, where he had built up a fleet. Alexios held him in check with the help of Taticios. Anna gives a dramatic description of the battle which took place at this time between two rival satraps, Sulayman and Tutush (Toutoush), brother of Grand Sultan Malik Shah, ruler of Jerusalem and Aleppo as far as Baghdad. In this battle the defeated Sulayman committed suicide, and the survivors of his forces joined those of Tutush. As Anna reports the accounts, the Seljuk sultan Malik Shah thought that his brother Tutush was growing too powerful, and he sent Alexios a letter with an envoy named Chaiuss, offering Alexios alliance by marriage to Anna, with the promise that he would drive all the satraps out of the maritime towns of the Byzantine Empire. Alexios resorted to strategy once again. He made no reference to the marriage alliance, leading Chaiuss to believe that he had no objection. Alexios convinced Chaiuss to accept baptism, follow the sultan's instructions by showing the letter to the satraps, then after expelling them, to return to the capital and become a

Byzantine subject. In this way, Chaiuss drove out all the satraps of the towns and returned to the capital, without Alexios lifting a finger or laying out a *nomisma* of his own. "After receiving holy baptism," Chaiuss received presents and "was appointed Duke of Anchialus" (VI, 9, p. 154).

When the suicide of Sulayman became known throughout the whole of Asia, each satrap governor over a town or fortress took that place and made it his own (VI, 10, p. 155). Abu'l Qasim, expecting to assume the dignity of a sultan, sent forth foraging parties to lay waste the whole of Bithynia as far as the Propontis. Alexios sent a considerable army headed by Taticios to Nicaea and a fleet headed by Manuel Butumites who set fire to Abu'l Qasim's fleet. The Latins helped make this a Roman victory, but Abu'l Qasim escaped. Alexios pursued him by letter, advising him to come over to the Romans, "for the enjoyment of bounteous gifts and honor" (VI, 10, p. 157). Abu'l Qasim dawdled for awhile but finally accepted Alexios's offer for peace and his invitation to the capital, where the emperor entertained him lavishly and sent him home by sea, in state, loaded with gifts (VI, 10, pp. 156-58).

When Prosuch besieged Nicaea with an army of fifty thousand men, Abu'l Qasim begged Alexios for aid, saying, according to Anna, that he preferred to be called the servant of Alexios than yield to Prosuch. Anna thought her father's decision to help Abu'l Qasim was a master stroke of strategy, for, as she explains, his plan was to help the weaker side. By so doing he might beat off the other side and then take the town from the former and make it his own. Alexios was not successful in this endeavor, despite his careful strategic planning, because the Roman forces were not strong enough to withstand an assault by the Turks, who were expected to join Prosuch, and so the Greeks returned to the capital (VI, 11, pp. 158-59).

Grand Sultan Malik Shah was still waiting for the return of Chaiuss. When he learned what had actually transpired, he sent Alexios a second letter, again offering a marriage alliance with Anna, but this time with his eldest son. He promised Alexios that if he would accept this marriage alliance, he would drive Abu'l Qasim out of Byzantine territory and all the other satraps out of Asia. But since Alexios sent troops to help Abu'l Qasim, the Sultan was unable to drive out the latter with his own troops. Abu'l Qasim, who did not want to lose his governorship of

Nicaea, decided to visit Sultan Malik Shah himself and took along fifteen mules loaded with gold and with gifts. Malik Shah would not even see Abu'l Qasim; instead he had him taken prisoner and strangled. All this while, Alexios allowed Malik Shah to think that he was still considering Anna's marriage with his son, but before Alexios's ambassadors even reached him, he heard of Malik Shah's murder. He had been killed by his brother Tutush when he heard that the sultan was negotiating peace with Alexios. Pergiaruch (Barkiyaruq), son of the murdered sultan, then killed Tutush, and Kilij Arslan (Anna calls him Clitziasthlan),[14] the elder of the two sons of the murdered Sulayman, was selected the new sultan.

Alexios now tried to regain two other coastal cities, Apollonias and Cyzicus, which had been taken by the Turks. In the first battle the Greeks met with defeat, but Alexios sent a second army which was victorious. He recaptured the territory along the coastal strip in the Sea of Marmora, including the city of Cyzicus. The Turkish archsatrap surrendered, and he and his blood relations accepted baptism, for Alexios, his daughter tells us, "was a real missionary by choice" (VI, 13, p. 164).

In 1086 Alexios was faced with another Scythian attack on the Roman Empire; the Scythians had crossed the Danube, ravaged the surrounding country, and taken a few small towns. In this battle the Scythians united with the Manichaeans, headed by Travlos, and Alexios was defeated. They returned in 1087, but this time Alexios summoned Taticios, and sent him with sufficient money to Adrianople to give the soldiers their pay for a year and to collect troops from all quarters so that he might raise a fresh army large enough for the war. This time the Romans returned victorious (VI, 14, p. 165-66).

In the spring of 1088 the Patzinaks plundered towns around Chariopolis with a mixed army and settled in a place called Scotinum. Alexios marched in person against them, remaining in Lardea for forty days and summoning troops on all sides. When the Patzinaks saw that George Euphorbenos was advancing with a large army and a fleet, and the emperor was marching toward them overland, they sent ambassadors to discuss terms of peace. Alexios, who recognized their treachery, refused to receive them, then resorted to ruse. He used an eclipse which was to take place that day as a sign from the heavens that the Scythians

were not sincere in their offers of peace. When the light of the
sun failed, the Scythians were terrified.[15] They were taken, but
the Scythians slew the guards and escaped (VII, 2, pp. 169-172).
In the autumn of the same year, another battle ensued with the
Scythians at Dristra, a town near the Danube. Despite the fact
that the Scythians worked havoc on the Byzantine army in this
battle, Anna writes with admiration of their plan of battle, "for
the science of warfare and ordering of troops is inbred in them"
(VII, 3, p. 174). The emperor himself stood in front of his army
holding a sword in one hand and the Pallium[16] of the Mother
of the Divine Word as a standard in the other, which actually
prevented him from "killing more Scythians." Alexios suffered
a terrific defeat in this battle; he was wounded and was nearly
captured himself. Only the quarrel between the Patzinaks and
the allies, the Cumans, resulting from a division of the spoils,
prevented the former from taking full advantage of their
victory. The emperor recuperated at Meroë and ransomed all the
captives.

The Cumans returned fully prepared to ally themselves with
Alexios against the Patzinaks, but the emperor had already concluded peace and had no need of them. However, the Patzinaks
broke their treaty; they seized Philippopolis and laid waste the
neighboring lands and cities. Alexios again negotiated for peace
with the Patzinaks, who accepted; but, writes Anna, "the inter-
val of peace with the Scythians did not last long, but like 'dogs
they returned to their vomit,'" and ravaged the neighboring
towns (VII, 6, p. 181). In the spring of 1089, the Patzinaks returned to Chariopolis and Alexios sent a band of "Archontopouli,"
a sacred band of soldiers who fell on the field much the same,
Anna tells us, "as the 'Sacred Band' of the Spartans in former
days."[17] The Patzinaks killed about three hundred men, over
whose loss the emperor shed bitter tears.

One Turkish invader who taxed Alexios more than any other
was Chaka (Tzachas), emir of Smyrna. Cleverly discerning the
manifold problems which Alexios faced, Chaka exploited the
Emperor's precarious position and began to menace the capital
from the south. Without much difficulty, Chaka took the town
of Clazomenae, Phocaea, Mitylene and Chios, and built a fleet
with native sailors. He devastated the islands he had captured
previously and entered into negotiations with the Scythians in

the north, advising them to seize the Chersonese, and with the Seljuks in Asia Minor in the east (VIII, 3, p. 198).

Alexios sent an adequate fleet and a land force under the leadership of Nicetas Castomonites, who was defeated. Chaka even carried off a number of the Roman ships. Alexios equipped a second fleet headed by Constantine Dalassenos. Chaka directed his course straight to Chios, and Dalassenos followed him. The Franks made an unsuccessful attempt to help the Romans in this battle, but Chaka sent them in headlong flight. Chaka, "who admired Dalassenos's brave and adventurous spirit," offered to discuss terms of peace with the Romans. When they met, Chaka explained the reasons for his hostility and offered a marriage alliance between a daughter of Alexios and one of his sons, after which he pledged to restore the islands he had taken. When told of this, Alexios regarded it as idle talk and sent John Ducas, his brother-in-law whom he had appointed great duke, with a fleet and land forces after Chaka, who had sailed secretly for Smyrna in order to collect more troops and then return to Chios (VII, 8, pp. 185-187). Dalassenos had a fierce conflict with the Turks while Chaka was still in Smyrna.

The five hundred horsemen promised by the count of Flanders arrived, and Alexios immediately sent them after Apelchasum, who was now starting on an expedition against Nicomedia. Alexios's genius as a strategist is seen when he instructs John Ducas not to battle at dawn against the sun's rays but to attack his adversaries "when the sun had passed the meridian and was inclining towards the west" (IX, 1, p. 215). John Ducas had been unsuccessful in his naval battle up to that time. The Byzantine fleet then defeated Chaka on the sea; Chaka sued for peace and stipulated that he should be allowed to sail to Smyrna unmolested, but as Anna says, "the crab never learns to walk straight." Chaka attacked again, was defeated again, though he himself escaped. After securing Mitylene, Ducas freed the islands still held by Chaka, took Samos and a few other islands, then returned to the capital. Chaka took possession of Smyrna (IX, 1, pp. 216-17). Again Alexios sent Constantine Dalassenos, now elected "Thalassocrator," after him. But now Alexios intrigued successfully to get Chaka's kinsman, Sultan Kilij Arslan, to murder him. The sultan met Chaka, greeted him cheerfully, invited him graciously to dine with him, got him drunk, and drove a sword into his side. The sultan and Alexios agreed on terms of peace and for a time calm was restored (IX, 3, p. 220).

The Patzinaks now arrived within twenty leagues of the capital and Alexios left Constantinople to do battle with them. Twice Neantzes, a deserter, betrayed the emperor's plan of attack to the Patzinaks; he was discovered, but, for some reason which Anna does not explain, Alexios simply dissembled his anger against Neantzes's treachery. The Roman army was completely routed. Alexios was obliged to retire to bed for a few days to recover from quartan fever (tetartaius pyritos) and chills, but again he led the attack against the Patzinaks; the Romans were victorious, and Alexios returned home to Constantinople.

After three days' rest, Alexios moved on to Tzouroulus to renew his battle against the Scythians. The emperor devised a most ingenious plan, which Anna describes. Her father requisitioned the wagons of the inhabitants and lifting the bodies from the wheels and axle trees, he suspended the latter from the battlements. Then he placed his troops on that side of the wall and instructed his men to cut the ropes which held them, when the Scythians reached the wall; thus the wheels and axles fell headlong on the Scythians. Alexios himself held the center of the line. The Scythians fled, and Alexios had a brilliant victory (VII, 11, pp. 191-93).

In 1091, only a week after Alexios had returned to the capital, he set out for Choerobacchi against the Patzinaks and met with success, which prompted him to play a joke on his men by dressing some of them in the garments of the Scythians. The heads of the Scythians were stuck on spears and carried aloft by other countrymen (VIII, 2, p. 196). Anna, who enjoys recalling her father's relationship with his men, and his humor, notes that her uncle Palaeologos who knew "how fertile in devices Alexios was immediately understood." However, she makes a point of telling us how disappointed her uncle was and how he complained bitterly and blamed himself for having been too late for the battle, "for he would have dearly liked to have had a share in that meed of fame" which her father had won. Alexios returned to Constantinople in triumph, but the Scythians continued to ravage all the provinces; they even came up to the villages in the neighborhood of the capital. Anna relates that on the day of the commemoration of the martyr Theodore, the inhabitants of the capital, who usually went in great numbers to the church of the martyr in a suburb beyond the city wall, did not even dare to open the gates of Byzantium, because the Patzinaks were standing under the walls (VIII, 3, p. 198).

An army of Cumans previously sent for by Alexios, approached the city, but Alexios, fearing that they might join with the Scythians, invited the Cuman chiefs to a conference, asked them to give him an oath and hostages, and bribed them into an alliance with him. Alexios wisely granted them permission to keep the whole booty they would take from the Patzinaks, if they were victorious. A band of about five thousand hardy mountaineers deserted to Alexios and offered him their services.

At Lebunium, the emperor no longer dissembled with the deserter Neantzes, but had him and his companions arrested and cast into irons. The Patzinaks made overtures to the Cumans, hoping to win them away from Alexios; they also sent envoys to the emperor to talk about peace. But, as Anna writes, her father had a fair idea of their double-dealings, and he kept them in suspense, especially since he was expecting "the arrival of the mercenary army from Rome" (VIII, 5, p. 202). On April 29, 1091, with the help of the Cumans, the Greeks defeated and annihilated the Patzinaks at Lebunium, so that for a time the Byzantine Empire was freed of Patzinak incursions. Anna credits her father with their disappearance; however, Byzantine historians all agree that the Patzinaks were finally exterminated by John II Comnenos in 1123. The Byzantines made a little song to celebrate that victory which said, "Just one day, the Scythians missed seeing the month of May" (VIII, 5, p. 205). One Byzantine historian notes that the interference of the Cumans in favor of Byzantium did an enormous service to the Christian world. "Their chiefs, Bonisk and Togorkhan, must be justly reckoned among the saviors of the Byzantine Empire."[18]

In 1094-95, the former allies, the Cumans, broke into Greek territory and advanced as far as Adrianople, plundering the countryside as they went. Their leader was a Byzantine pretender who claimed to be Constantine Diogenes (killed in Antioch), son of Emperor Romanos IV, who had been married to Theodora, Alexios's sister. Alexios went in person to Adrianople, selected a large body of Turks, and launched them against the Cumans. Alexios overcame the Cumans and returned victorious to the capital (X, 2, 3, 4, pp. 238-47).

After a short rest Alexios discovered that the Turks were over-running the interior of Bithynia and plundering everything. Anna describes her father's strategic device which fenced off Bithynia with a canal against the incursions of the Turks. Anna never completed that story because of the approach of the innumerable armies of the Crusaders (X, 5, p. 247, 248).

The last years of Alexios were occupied with fresh struggles against the Turks. When the emperor learned that the Turks had besieged Nicaea, he went to Lopadium to await the arrival of his troops and the mercenary army he had hired. He then moved to Nicomedia where he enrolled recruits and trained them. He began his attack against the Turks at Nicaea; but when he learned that the Turks had set fire to all the crops and plains in Asia, Alexios feared that his men would fall prey to famine and he did not know how to proceed. From Anna's account her father put two questions on two pieces of paper and set them on the Holy Table from which a priest picked one, and this decided Alexios to attack around Philomelium. He took Philomelium by assault and defeated the Turks, who then sued for peace; Alexios made them presents of a very large sum of money and sent them away well satisfied (XV, 4, p. 399, p. 401; 6, p. 406).

In 1114, an invasion by the Cumans summoned Alexios to Philippopolis, but they disappeared when they heard that the emperor himself led the attack. Anna ends her report on the Turks by remarking that her father "considered it a species of victory that by the mere sound of his name he had driven the barbarians away" (XIV, 9, p. 387).

Anna's account of her father's struggle is on the whole reliably told. As is to be expected, she softens her father's defeats and highlights his victories. It cannot be denied, however, that she gives credit to the intelligence and bravery of this formidable enemy which was the final victor of the Byzantine Empire.

III   *The Struggle of Alexios Against the Normans*

... in the west things were very bad, as Robert was letting out every reef in his endeavor to foist that Pseudo-Michael, who had appealed to him, upon the throne. (III, 9, p. 89)

Anna regards the Norman invasion as infinitely more trying on her father, despite the frequent incursions of the Turks, most likely because both Anna and her father thought of the Latins as fellow Christians. "By them," Anna writes of the Normans, "the Emperor was engulfed in an immense sea of worries, for he had long grasped the fact that the Franks were dreaming of the Roman Empire" (XIV, 4, 2, p. 372).

Anna informs the reader that her information came from a certain Latin, an envoy from the bishop of Bari who had assisted at the expedition of Guiscard (III, 12, p. 97). Chalandon sees so striking a resemblance between certain passages in the *Alexiad* and the corresponding passages in the Latin chronicle of William of Apulia, which led him to believe that Anna had utilized that Latin source, or else the oral accounts furnished by the Latin envoy. He also believes that Anna used the military correspondence of her father, as well as his diplomatic correspondence with foreign sovereigns.[19]

What is most striking in Anna's account of the Norman invasion is her colorful characterization of the adversaries who led the invasion, and her dramatic account of the battles they fought. Robert Guiscard is the malevolent protagonist in the Norman invasion. "Normandy indeed begot him," she writes, "but he was nursed and reared by consummate Wickedness" (I, 10, p. 26). He was a man "in temper tyrannical, in mind most cunning, brave in action ... most obstinate in achievement." Of his appearance she writes that, "his stature was so lofty that he surpassed even the tallest . . . his eyes all but emitted sparks of fire . . . his cry put thousands to flight" (I, 10, p. 27). Of his son Bohemond (whom Anna calls Saniscus)[20] she writes that he "took after his father in all things, in audacity, bodily strength, bravery, and untamable temper . . . these two, father and son, might rightly be termed 'the caterpillar and the locust' for whatever escaped Robert, that his son Behemond took to him and devoured" (I, 14, pp. 37-38). About Robert's amazon wife Gaita, who accompanied her husband, Anna writes, "when dressed in full armor, the woman was a fearsome sight" (I, 15, p. 38).

As for the invasion itself, we learn from Anna that in May 1081, one month after Alexios had been proclaimed emperor, Robert Guiscard crossed the Adriatic with his son Roger, thirty thousand men and one hundred and fifty ships, intending to invade Dyrrachium, regarded as the key to Byzantium in the west. He had already captured Valona and the strongly fortified island of Corfu (I, 16, p. 40). As soon as Alexios learned of this he left the capital in charge of his mother and went after

Guiscard himself. As has already been stated elsewhere, Robert's excuse for war was the annulment of his daughter's betrothal to Constantine Ducas when his father Michael VII was deposed by Nicephoros Botaneiates. Anna gives us a vivid scene of Robert in Dyrrachium with a monk named Raictor posing as the deposed Michael. Robert had dressed Raictor in magnificent robes and exhibited him before the inhabitants of Dyrrachium. When they did not recognize him as the emperor Michael, they "poured down a stream of insults upon him"; Robert, however, paid no heed to these insults; he continued to use this as an excuse for war. Actually, this was a pretext for his own ambition to seize the Byzantine throne (IV, 1, p. 99).

In the meantime George Palaeologos had arrived in Dyrrachium. When Robert heard of this, he made careful preparations for a siege by building turrets on his ships. Anna speaks of horses and fully equipped cavalry which Robert embarked on his cruisers, since his plan was to surround Dyrrachium with battering engines on land and sea. At Butrinto (Buthrotum) he joined forces with his son Bohemond and divided his army in two, one part of which sailed with him to Dyrrachium, while the other marched overland to Dyrrachium with Bohemond. Robert was caught in a severe storm, which appears to Anna "as if God were pouring out his wrath upon Robert's insolent and overweening presumptuousness." He lost men and provisions; but when he had buried the dead with due rites, he collected his whole army from land and sea and occupied the plain of Illyria (III, 12, pp. 96-97).

George Palaeologos, who led the counterattack against Robert, also began to fortify the city. He built bulwarks, then rushed out to meet the foe. Despite a severe wound, he continued fighting with "untiring industry." Alexios realized that the forces which he had at his command were only a small fraction of Robert's. Since he knew that he would be unable to overcome the invader with his own limited forces, he called on the Turks in the east for help, and on the Venetians. He also wrote a letter to the king of Germany, which Anna quotes in full (pp. 91-92), in which he proposed alliance and marriage between Isaac's son and his daughter. He also sent letters to Hermanus,[21] Duke of Lombardy, the pope of Rome, and the archbishop of Capua, promising great gifts and dignities to "incite them to war against Robert." Alexios replaced the treacherous Monomachatos, then governor of Dyrrachium, with his brother-in-law George Palaeologos, which finally opened the way for him to sign a peace treaty with the Turks (III, 10, pp. 91-92; 12, p. 95).

That summer, Robert, accompanied by his wife Sigelgaita, and his ablest son Bohemond, laid siege to Dyrrachium. At first, when the Venetians saw Robert's well-fitted fleet, they lost heart. When night fell, however, the Venetians made elaborate preparations, constructing a "sea-harbor," building wooden towers at their mastheads, placing armed men in small boats and putting up heavy beams studded with sharp nails, waiting for the approach of the Frankish fleet (IV, 2, p. 101).

In the fierce battle which followed, the Venetians knocked a hole into Bohemond's ship, which put the Norman in imminent danger and he had to leap to another boat in order to save his life. The Venetians routed the enemy and pursued them to Robert's camp where they started another battle. George Palaeologos, who held the citadel of Dyrrachium, rushed out and fought on the side of the Venetians. The Byzantines, with the help of the Venetians, were victorious in this battle. Alexios received the Venetians with great honor for this tremendous victory (IV, 2, p. 101).

Another bitter battle ensued during which Robert's men fled. This decided Robert to "haul up his whole fleet" and wait for two months near the harbor of Hiericho while he made new preparations to continue the war. Robert could do nothing because the Roman and Venetian fleets were guarding the straits; he could get no provisions, even from the mainland, and his men began to suffer from hunger. "In the course of three months," concludes Anna, "a total of ten thousand men are said to have perished" (IV, 3, p. 102).

From Anna's description, Robert was no less a clever strategist than her father; he, too, in her words, "had an inventive mind" and was a "deep thinker." She tells us that when Robert discovered that the river was almost dried up by the drought, he fixed posts along either side, had large trees cut down which he laid flat, and strewed sand over them so that the water was collected and flowed together into one spot. Gradually, the water formed pools and filled the whole bed of the river until they could float (IV, 3, pp. 102-3).

When Alexios heard about Robert's ingenious preparations, he himself set out at once from Constantinople, leaving Isaac in the

capital to take care of things.[22] In Robert's second attack against
Dyrrachium, George Palaeologos was severely wounded, but he
continued to fight bravely until evening. Both men built towers;
Robert outside the walls of Dyrrachium, George Palaeologos
inside, bombarding Robert with a volley of darts. When Alexios
arrived, he sent envoys to Robert to find out why the Norman
was fighting him. Robert's verbal reply repeated what he had
been saying all along; it was to "avenge the injustice done to
my kinsman in marriage." Robert was willing to end the war,
providing Alexios was ready "to fulfill the conditions" which his
ambassadors had signified to him. "These requests," writes Anna,
"were absolutely impossible and injurious" (IV, 5, p. 106).

Alexios arranged for his native army to make a sudden night
attack on Robert's entrenchments from the rear. He himself
intended to attack Robert from the front as soon as other troops
arrived. The Venetian vessels relieved Dyrrachium at sea, but the
land forces, "the barbarian troops," consisting of Macedonian
Slavs, Turks, the imperial Varangian English bodyguard, and
some other nationalities, were heavily defeated. The few who
escaped found refuge in the chapel of Saint Michael, "but,"
writes Anna, "the Latins started a fire and burnt them down,
chapel and all." The rest of the Roman army fought bravely,
but Robert drove back the Roman phalanx and split it into frag-
ments (IV, 6, p. 109). Oman states that the Varangians were
carried away by their eagerness to begin the fray. Alexios's
main body was too far away to turn all his forces against the
Normans, and they were cut to pieces before the main body
had reached the field. The rest of Alexios's army came into action
only after the Varangians had been destroyed.[23] Alexios himself, who lingered last on the field and was surrounded, escaped
only by the speed of his horse and the strength of his sword arm.

Robert sent his strongest men in pursuit of the emperor, overtook him and thrust him with spears. "It was Divine Providence," writes Anna, that aided her father, for his horse "suddenly leapt through the air and stood on top of a hill." Robert
censured his men sharply when they returned to his encampment without Alexios (IV, 7, p. 112-113). When the inhabitants,
the majority of whom were colonists from Amalfi and
Venice, learned of Robert's intention to renew the siege of
Dyrrachium the following spring, they opened their gates to
the Norman and surrendered the city to him. Alexios allowed

himself a short rest at Achrida, then sent for his remaining followers to assemble at Thessalonika. Alexios now proceeded to train new recruits (V, 1, pp. 115-16). His whole mind was intent on retrieving this defeat.

Robert returned to Italy in 1082 because "the king of Alamania had all but arrived in Lombardy." From what Anna writes, this had been engineered by Alexios himself; he had sent ambassadors to the king of Alamania (Henry IV of Germany) so that he could get Robert out of Byzantium and give him a chance to reassemble his army and collect foreign troops while Robert was occupied there (V, 3, pp. 119-120).

Before Robert left he handed over the command to his son Bohemond, who occupied Dyrrachium, Valona, and all the remaining towns won by his father. Soon after, Bohemond marched through Bagenetia to Joannina, set up his tent inside the town, and sent out raiding parties to plunder the surrounding country and towns. Alexios left Constantinople in May and arrived in Joannina. Since he recognized that his forces were inferior to Robert's, he decided to attack with missiles made by a small picked body of peltasts. He also had wagons built and filled these with heavy infantry to break the line of the Latins when they "came dashing down at full gallop." Then Alexios drew up his regiments in order of battle and he himself took command of the center. But Bohemond avoided the wagons, "as if he had fore-knowledge of it," and attacked the Roman ranks on either flank. Anna concedes that Bohemond carried off the victory (V, 4, p. 123).

Alexios then reassembled his regiments and started again on his march against Bohemond with a new device to overcome the Franks. "But," writes Anna, "whatever plans my father made against him in the evening, the Franks knew by the morning" (V, 4, p. 124). Evidently, Alexios learned of this leak of information before it was too late, for Anna says her father "skillfully modified his plans." But the Roman lines were thrown into utter confusion anyway in the hand-to-hand battle that followed, and Alexios himself was wounded. When the emperor saw that his whole army had disappeared, he decided to flee from danger and return to the capital. Anna expresses one of her basic beliefs as she excuses her father's defeat: "when anyone after heavy travail has no longer the strength to make a stand against his

enemies, he would be a fool if he thrust himself into certain
danger" (V, 4, p. 124).

When Alexios reached the capital, he asked the Sultan for
troops and experienced generals. The sultan complied and sent
Alexios seven thousand men with highly experienced leaders
whom the emperor planned to use in his next attack on
Bohemond. In the meantime, the Franks took Pelagonia, Trik-
kala, and Castoria. Bohemond himself entered Tzibiscus; then
he approached Larissa and started to besiege it. The inhabitants
of Larissa put up a stout resistance for six months. However
Alexios could not start on his march against Bohemond immediately, because he was recruiting mercenaries from all
quarters. He finally reached the territory close to Larissa and
studied the topography of the land, as he always did, so he
could set up ambuscades near Larissa, where he pitched his
camp. But he knew that the struggle would be a difficult one
because Bohemond's forces were superior. Anna tells us that a
vision which appeared in his sleep told him not to grieve, that he
would conquer, which lifted his spirits. The next day he decided
to entrust all his divisions and the royal standards to his relatives.
While the emperor was giving orders, all the horses started to
neigh, which Anna tells us was also regarded as a good omen
(V, 5, 127-28).

Alexios prepared an ambush which deceived Bohemond and led
him away from his encampment; he and his men then headed
for Bohemond's encampment with a number of Franks and
carried off the booty before going after the pursuers of his own
men. They overtook the Franks and showered arrows upon
their horses. "For every Frank is invincible both in attack and
appearance when he is on horseback," Anna observes, "but when
he comes off his horse, partly due to the size of his shield, and
partly to the long curved peaks of his shoes and a consequent
difficulty in walking, then he becomes very easy to deal with and
a different man altogether, for all his mental energy evaporates,
as it were" (V, 6, p. 129). In the battle of Larissa, the Greeks
inflicted a severe defeat upon the Normans, which forced them
back to Epirus.

Alexios again used ruse successfully by sending offers of
rich rewards to the counts in Bohemond's train, on condition that
they would ask Bohemond for the pay he had promised them,
which they hadn't received for four years. He urged them to

persuade Bohemond to journey down to the sea himself to fetch it. Bohemond returned to Lombardy, and Alexios returned to the capital in triumph (V, 7, pp. 131-32).

Bohemond left for Italy in 1083, but he returned with his father the following year with a large force and mercenary troops collected in Europe; "horse and foot," writes Anna, "all splendidly equipped and eager for action" (VI, 5, p. 144). He also sent for his sons Roger and Guido; Alexios tried unsuccessfully to separate Guido from his father by "promises of high preferment and an extravagant sum of money." Robert and his sons took Buthrotum at the first assault. Then Robert left his sons there and sailed with his whole fleet to Corfu, which had revolted again.

Alexios now urged the Venetians to furnish a large fleet; he himself equipped biremes, triremes, and piratical vessels with hoplites skilled in naval warfare. Robert was defeated three times, but the Venetians and Romans lost the fourth battle to Bohemond. As Anna evaluates the causes of that defeat, the Venetians must have been overelated by their previously gained victories. Robert and his son destroyed the Venetian fleet off Corfu. However, the Venetian fleet equipped itself again and gained a great victory over Bohemond in their next battle.

In the spring of 1084, Alexios returned to Castoria, which was still held by the Franks, and made an assault on the towers and walls with his battering machines. Then he made war from land and from the lake. Some of the Franks deserted to the emperor, while the Frank Bryennios, count of Brienne and constable of Apulia, took an oath never to take arms against the emperor again, on condition that the emperor would grant him safe conduct to the frontier and let him return to his own country. Alexios returned triumphantly to the capital.

The war ended only when Robert died in the north of the island of Cephalonia in 1085 of an epidemic which broke out among his troops. With Robert's death the Norman invasion of Byzantine territory ended, and Dyrrachium was returned to the Greeks. But as Vasiliev points out, "even today a small bay and village in the Island, Fiscardo (Guiscardo, Portus Wiscardi, in the Middle Ages, from the name of Robert Guiscard) recalls the name of the powerful Duke of Apulia."[24]

Chalandon states that Robert Guiscard "opened a new way to the ambition of his descendants; after him the Italian Normans were to turn their gaze toward the East at the expense of the

Greek Empire. Twelve years later Bohemond will dream of creating a principality for himself."[25] Vasiliev notes (pp. 381-82) that Venice, in return for the aid given by her fleet, established the Republic of St. Mark, a very profitable position in the Byzantine Empire, and a solid foundation for the power of Venice in the East.

IV *The First Crusade*

Before he had enjoyed even a short rest, he heard a report of the approach of innumerable Frankish armies. (*Alexiad*, X, 5, 2, p. 248)

In no other report in Anna's history can it be said more truly that the *Alexiad* is a panegyric to her father than in her report of the First Crusade. In no other report in her history do we become aware of both her strength as a historian, and of her inaccuracies and omissions, as we do when we read her Hellenic eyewitness account of the crusaders who swooped on Byzantine soil in May, 1096. Anna's is the only Greek account we have of the First Crusade; for this reason it merits careful study. On the whole, her report on the crusaders is the same as that of the Latin chroniclers; it is her causes and effects and the emphasis she gives to each which vary.

Anna's statement given above would indicate that the arrival of the crusaders came as a complete surprise to her father. She did record that her father had asked the Count of Flanders for help against the Patzinak attacks when the latter visited the emperor on his way to Jerusalem. She also noted that her father expected soldiers from Rome in 1091. Both of these requests, however, were made five years before the arrival of the crusaders in Byzantium.

From other sources we learn that her father had cordial relations with Urban II even before he made these requests. In 1089, Urban II lifted the excommunication which had been imposed on Alexios by Gregory VII; as a result of this, the Latin churches in Constantinople reopened.[26] In 1090, Alexios sent an embassy to Urban II bearing messages of cordial friendship.[27] He also wrote to Urban II for aid when discussing the union of the churches.[28] In 1095, Alexios sent ambassadors to the Council of Piacenza, again to ask for aid.[29] For whatever reason Anna may have had, she omitted all mention of her father's cordial relations with Urban II. In fact, the name of Urban II never appears in the *Alexiad*. The question is: to what extent was Alexios directly responsible for the First Crusade?

Most Byzantine scholars agree with Anna and state that Alexios did not ask for a crusade. What the emperor requested was aid to raise troops from the west in order to drive the Turks out of Asia. Runciman asserts that at the Council of Piacenza, to which Alexios sent his ambassadors, the emperor hoped to get "small companies" of recruits; he never expected entire Frankish armies. And the fact that Urban insisted on Constantinople as the meeting place of the crusaders certainly makes it appear that the pope was confident that Alexios would welcome it.[30] Chalandon also believes that the news of the First Crusade came to Alexios as a complete and disconcerting surprise because he neither expected nor desired assistance in the form of a crusade.[31] Vasiliev states that if Alexios appealed for aid at Piacenza, he did not dream of crusading armies; he wanted mercenaries to fight the Turks who had made a successful advance in Asia Minor.[32]

Charanis does not agree with this; he holds Alexios, along with Urban II, as the instigators of the First Crusade, and he gives convincing evidence from both Latin and Greek contemporary sources to substantiate his point of view. Since Constantinople was fixed as the meeting place of the crusading armies, is it possible that Alexios would not have received some official notice from the pope concerning the arrival of the crusaders at the Byzantine capital? Charanis quotes from a contemporary source which speaks "of an embassy sent by Urban II to Alexios I in order to inform the latter of the deliberation of the Council of Clermont."[33] He agrees with other Byzantine scholars that the real reason for Alexios's request for aid from the west was to drive the Turks out of Asia Minor; he also admits that Alexios never expected a crusade as it was conceived and organized by Urban II.[34] The point of difference which this Byzantine scholar stresses is that "in the plea for help which the Byzantine ambassadors made at Piacenza, they put the emphasis on the necessity of liberating the Holy Lands."[35] He also refers to a contemporary Latin source written by Bernold, who states that "the embassy which appeared before Urban II on March 17, 1095, 'humbly beseeched' the Pope . . . to procure for him some help against the pagans for the defense of the holy church." Bernold goes on to say that the pope reacted favorably to Alexios's request and engaged the crusaders to go to the aid of Alexios.[36] In the Greek contemporary source to which Charanis refers, the author Skutariotes states that Alexios craftily instructed his ambassadors at Piacenza to say that the Byzantine Empire "considered unbearable the domination of Jerusalem and the life-giving Sepulchre of Our Savior Jesus Christ by the Persians"; they prevailed "over not a few of them to leave their country and succeeded in directing them in every way to the task."[37]

Munro, who studied the speech of Pope Urban II at Clermont, also states that the pope devoted a part of his speech to the appeals Alexios had made to him. Munro quotes Sybel who asserts that Alexios's appeal at the Council of Piacenza was "the final impulse" which caused the First Crusade.[38] In light of the above evidence, it would seem that the crusaders were not as unexpected as Anna states. From what we know of Alexios as a strategist, he must have instructed his ambassadors to exploit the Christian duty of the council for his own political ends. Urban II must have connected the union of the churches with the crusade.

Anna is also shocked over the countless numbers of crusaders who arrived on Byzantine territory. She writes: "the whole of the West and all the barbarian tribes which dwell between the further side of the Adriatic and the pillars of Hercules had all migrated into Asia" (X, 5, p. 248). She gives fantastic figures for every contingent which reached Constantinople. The evidence of Ekkehard quoted by Charanis states that Alexios urged Urban II to call to his aid the entire occident.[39] However, Runciman advises the reader of the *Alexiad* to divide Anna's figures by ten; he estimates that "in all from sixty to one hundred thousand persons entered the Empire from the West between the summer of 1096 and the spring of 1097."[40]

By far the most successfully achieved part in Anna's report of the First Crusade is her dramatic portrayal of the remarkable way Alexios handled the vexing confrontations instigated by the crusaders, without any rupture in their relations. Nowhere does she portray her father to greater advantage as a political diplomat, as a calm and restrained ruler, and as a military strategist as she does in this section of her history.

She tells us that her father granted audiences to the Franks starting from daybreak. They filed to the palace unannounced to make their requests; they even invaded the emperor's bathroom to annoy him. They would not let him eat his breakfast undisturbed; fatigued as he was in the evening, without having eaten all day, they still followed him into his private bedroom at night to ask for money or a favor or advice, or even nothing better than idle chatter; yet, "you could see him all alone and with unchanging countenance ever giving a ready answer to all their questions" (XIV, 4, 3, p. 373). Alexios used all the finesse of the Byzantine diplomat, all the adroitness of the strategist, to appease the Latin counts, giving them tents full of money, supplying them wih provisions for their armies, and distributing gifts and dignities for the help he needed to recover the regions he had lost to the Turks.

Alexios knew the character of the Norman invader even before his ascension to the throne. For this reason, as his daughter states, the emperor "dreaded their arrival for he knew their irresistible manner of attack, their unstable and mobile character and all the concomitant characteristics which the Frank retains throughout" (X, 5, 2, p. 248). Despite his dread of the Franks, however, Alexios immediately prepared to receive the crusaders in the manner of an extravagantly rich and welcoming host. He sent leaders to Dyrrachium and Valona, along with interpreters who could speak Latin, with instructions to welcome the Franks courteously and to provide them with provisions; but as a precautionary measure, he also instructed his envoys to keep an eye on them, covertly, and if they should see them "making any foraging excursions, they were to come out from undercover and check them by light skirmishing" (X, 5, p. 250).

As Anna describes their arrival, great hordes of locusts preceded each successive arrival of Latin contingents, which left the wheat untouched but destroyed the vines; diviners interpreted this to mean that the Franks would not injure the Christians but attack the sensuous Ismaelites (X, 5, 2, p. 249). She then gives us vivid descriptions of the arrival of each contingent.

Peter the Hermit was the first to reach Byzantium. Anna erroneously credits Peter for having organized the First Crusade, probably because of an association to his earlier unsuccessful trip to Jerusalem. She also erroneously calls him a bishop. Although she came to look upon Peter as a "haughty Latin," she did not confuse his religious motives with those of the Frankish counts who were bent on capturing the Byzantine throne. She believed that "Peter for his part undertook his journey originally only to worship at the Holy Sepulchre" (X, 9, p. 258). From what

she writes, Alexios had known about Peter's earlier trip to the
Holy Land and of his sufferings at the hands of the Turks, and
he was particularly anxious to make Peter's second trip more
successful. Chalandon doubts whether Alexios spoke to Peter
about his first trip to Jerusalem, as Anna states.[41] Anna was
annoyed when Peter refused to heed her father's advice to wait
for the arrival of the counts before proceeding on his way to
Jerusalem but listened to his followers instead. She does not
explain how it was that about ten thousand of Peter's men
had been separated. She writes that these men "devastated the
country around Nicaea and behaved most cruelly to all. They
dismembered some of the children and fixed others on wooden
spits and roasted them at the fire, and on persons advanced in
age they inflicted every kind of torture" (X, 6, p. 251). The
author of the *Gesta Francorum* also mentions the devastation
and massacre caused by Peter's men. He states that Peter the
Hermit's men "did not cease doing all manner of evil, burning
and plundering houses and churches."[42]

As a result of this massacre, a violent conflict ensued between
the Turks in Nicaea. Peter's men overcame the Turks, then took
all their booty and returned to Helenopolis where they had first
pitched camp. Again some of Peter's men separated and marched
to Xerigordus, which they took by assault. The sultan dispatched
Elchanes with a substantial force against the crusaders; the sultan
was out to get Peter the Hermit and his whole army; he placed
ambushes and tricked the Franks into believing that they had
captured Nicaea and were now dividing the loot. "Directly they
heard the words 'partition' and 'money,'" writes Anna, "they
started in a disorderly crowd along the road to Nicaea, all
but unmindful of their military experience and the discipline
which is essential for those starting out to battle" (X, 6, p. 251).
The Franks were almost annihilated in the conflict, which Anna
believes would have been avoided had Peter taken her father's
advice. Peter himself managed to escape with a few of his
followers and they reentered Helenopolis.

When Alexios heard of this unfortunate attack on Peter, he
sent a large force embarked on ships of war to Peter's aid. When
the Turks saw them land, they fled. Anna again points out that
her father did not want the crusaders to become a prey to the
Turkish sword because he cared for them as Christians. Peter and
his followers were finally brought safely to the capital. When

Alexios rebuked Peter for not taking his advice, the hermit blamed it on the other Franks and denounced them as robbers and plunderers. Despite this, the emperor received him kindly and supplied Peter's army with provisions. Later, Peter rebuked his men, who were suffering from hunger and were blockaded by the Turks, for they were not keeping themselves pure; he exhorted them to find the Lance,[43] which Anna calls the Holy Nail, although Christians and Muslims generally refer to it as the Lance. The Franks found it, and then entrusted it to Isangeles (Raymond Count of St. Giles) to carry it in battle "as he was the holiest of them all" This inspired the crusaders with new courage.

This is all that Anna tells us about Peter the Hermit and his undisciplined followers. She neglects to tell us about the attack of the Patzinaks on Peter when he and his army forced their way across the Sava River; nor does she tell us that, when Peter and his army entered Belgrade, they pillaged and set fire to the city. Peter's hordes committed great ravages, plundering their way through Hungary and the Balkans. Alexios sent ambassadors to meet Peter before the entrance at Sofia. Oman throws the blame on the crusaders as the instigators, for, as he states, "the newcomers pillaged his country right and left upon their way, and were drawn into many bloody fights with the peasantry and the imperial garrisons which might have ended in open war. But Alexios set himself to work to smooth matters down; all his tact and patience were needed."[44]

Hugh, count of Vermandois (whom Anna calls Ubus), brother of the king of France, was the next to arrive. He preceded his arrival with a ridiculous message to Alexios ordering him to prepare a magnificent reception for him, and announcing that he was "the king of kings and the greatest of those under heaven" (X, 7, p. 253). Yet Alexios took Hugh's arrogance in stride; he sent John Comnenos, Duke of Dyrrachium, and Nicholas Mavrocatacalon, Duke of the Fleet, to be on the look-out for his arrival and to receive Hugh with all due ceremony. When Hugh arrived safely at the seaboard of Lombardy, he sent twenty-four ambassadors "protected with cuirasses and greaves of gold" to the Duke of Dyrrachium, announcing that he was the leader of the Frankish army, and that he was bringing with him from Rome the golden standard of Saint Peter. The duke was to prepare a reception for him and his forces which would be

worthy of his royal blood and to meet him in person. During the
crossing Hugh was caught in a severe storm; he lost the greater
number of vessels, though he himself was saved. When Hugh
finally arrived on a horse borrowed from one of Alexios's men
who were on the lookout for him, the duke received him with
great ceremony, set a rich banquet before him, notified the
emperor of his arrival, and "detained him and left him, not
without supervision, but certainly free," then waited for further
instructions from the emperor. Alexios sent Butumites to escort
Hugh to the capital. The emperor received Hugh with all honor,
showed him much friendliness, gave him a large sum of money,
showered him with presents, and persuaded him to swear the
oath of fealty customary to the Latins (X, 7, p. 254). Alexios
knew that in the West allegiance was established by solemn
oath, and he decided to demand such an oath from all the
counts; they were to return any territory they conquered which
had formerly belonged to the Byzantine Empire. For the service
they were to give Alexios as mercenaries, he would lavish on
them gifts and money, and such luxuries as they had never
known. Hugh, dazzled by the extravagant wealth and by the
generosity of the emperor, was easily persuaded to take the
oath.

Close on his heels came the count of Prebentza (Provence).
According to Anna, this count arrived in a pirate vessel. Nicolas
Mavrocatacalon, Duke of the Roman fleet, went after him and
caught him as he was hurrying towards the opposite coast of
Dyrrachium. The Latins attacked the Roman fleet with the
crossbow, "quite unknown to the Greeks" and "a devilish inven-
tion." The battle lasted from evening until the next midday, and
then "the Latins surrendered much against their will, after asking
and obtaining a promise of immunity" (X, 8, pp. 254-57).

Now Count Godfrey of Bouillon, duke of Lower Lorraine,
"very rich and very proud of his bravery, courage and conspicuous lineage," arrived and quartered his army near the
Propontis. Alexios urged him to cross the Straits of the Propontis,
but Godfrey postponed doing so on one pretext after another,
Anna says. As she surmises, "he was waiting for the arrival of
Bohemond and the rest of the Counts" (X, 9, p. 258). In the
meantime, the emperor invited some of the counts with Godfrey
to take the oath.

A false rumor reached the others that the counts were prisoners at Constantinople, whereupon Count Godfrey moved his regiments, laying waste the country until he reached the walls of Constantinople. Albert of Aix states that Alexios "sent 500 Turcopoles who shot the soldiers of the Duke; it was then that Godfrey's men set fire to the buildings and caused irreparable damage to Constantinople. After sunrise the next day, Godfrey's men wandered about plundering the lands of the kingdom for six days."[45] Anna writes that the emperor had to send troops to compel Godfrey to cross the Straits. Alexios insisted that not a single person should go out of the city to fight the Latins because it was Good Friday, and because he wanted to avoid civil disturbance. Not only did the Latins disobey the emperor's order, but they even placed more troops and sent heavy showers of arrows. Alexios sent for Nicephoros Bryennios and instructed him to shoot arrows, but not to hit, in order to terrify the Latins. Finally, the emperor was forced to throw in his own troops, and the Franks were finally worsted.

Shortly after this Godfrey took the oath of fealty to deliver to the emperor whatever towns, countries, or forts he would take which had formerly belonged to the Roman Empire. After Godfrey took the oath, Alexios gave him a large sum of money and invited him to his table where he feasted luxuriously; then Godfrey crossed the straits and encamped near Pelecanus. Alexios gave orders that abundant supplies of food should be sent to them (X, 9, p. 261).

After this Count Raoul arrived and he also bivouacked by the Propontis. Alexios sent Opus overland to Raoul with orders to compel him to cross the straits. When Raoul would not obey the emperor's order, Opus drew up his lines for battle, and Raoul entered into the fight "like a lion that has lighted upon a huge carcass." Pegasius, who had come to transport the Franks, disembarked and attacked the Franks from the rear. "In this battle," Anna writes, "many were killed but a far greater number wounded." Alexios put the survivors on boats and transported them to Constantinople; to the Counts he sent envoys with friendly greetings and promises of great expectations, consequently on arrival they took the oath (X, 10, p. 262).

After Raoul came another innumerable heterogeneous crowd, Anna tells us, collected from nearly all the Frankish countries together with their leaders. Again the emperor sent men to receive them hospitably, to convey pledges of reasonable assistance, to supply them with provisions for their journey (X, 10, 3, p. 262).

The following day Alexios summoned the counts and sent for Godfrey from Pelecanus, so he would be present during the taking of the oath. Anna relates that after the oath had been taken, one of the boorish Franks sat on the emperor's seat. Her father said nothing to this, but Baldwin rebuked the Frank for his boorishness, not only because they had just sworn fealty to the emperor, but also because this was against the customs of the country. Muttering to himself, the Frank called Alexios a rustic who sat while the Frankish counts were left standing. Alexios had one of his men translate what the Frank had said, but still Alexios said nothing. When, however, it was time for them to leave, Alexios asked the Frank who he was. When the Frank boasted that he was one of the "purest nobility" and that no antagonist had ever dared to fight him, Alexios warned him that now he would meet an antagonist in the Turk, but he advised him how to fight if he wished to survive (X, 3, pp. 263-64).

Bohemond crossed fifteen days later without a large force, Anna says, owing to his poverty. Bohemond was known to Alexios, of course, long before this, as a "treacherous and scheming" person. Alexios used all his tact, diplomacy, and wit to persuade Bohemond to cross into Asia before the others so that he would not "corrupt their minds also."

Despite Anna's passionate hatred of Bohemond, she gives us an epic description of the Frank whom her father regarded as his worst enemy. According to her, Bohemond was a marvel to behold. He was extremely tall, narrow waisted, broad shouldered, had powerful hands and arms, yet perfectly proportioned. He had a very white skin; his yellow hair was cut short, unlike the other knights, and he was smooth shaven. For the dark-eyed Anna, Bohemond's "blue eyes indicated both a high spirit and dignity." But she also thinks that his charm was partly marred by a general air of the horrible (XIII, 10, 2, p. 347).

Anna states that Bohemond took the oath of fealty without any hesitation whatever. The author of the *Gesta Francorum* states that Alexios said "that, if he willingly took the oath to him, he would give him, in return, land in extent from Antioch fifteen days' journey, and eight in width."[46] According to Anna, Alexios offered him a room full of riches, which he accepted at first, then refused petulantly, finally changed his mind and accepted. Alexios prepared lodging and a meal for Bohemond, but the Frank gave the meal to his attendants. Later, when he discovered that nothing had happened to his attendants, he confessed that he feared Alexios was arranging his death by mixing poison with his food. When Bohemond demanded the office of Great Domestic of the East (Commander-in-chief of all the imperial forces in Asia), Alexios shrewdly put him off by saying, "the time for that has not come yet; but by your energy and reputation and above all by your fidelity it will come ere long" (X, 11, p. 267).

Anna singled out Count Isangeles, a deeply religious man known as Raymond Count of St. Giles, whom her father liked especially because of his "superior wisdom and genuine sincerity, purity, and because he valued truth above everything" (X, 11, p. 267). Alexios retained Isangeles after the other counts had left to confide in him his suspicions of the Frank's intentions but especially to ask him to be on the alert against Bohemond's wickedness and to check him should Bohemond break his oath. As Anna reports, to this confidence Isangeles replied: "Bohemond has acquired perjury and treachery as a species of ancestral heritage, and it would be a miracle, if he kept his oath. However, I will endeavor as far as in me lies always to carry out your orders" (X, 11, p. 268). There is no evidence in the *Alexiad* that he ever rebuked Bohemond for violating his oath.

Anna makes a very unconvincing attempt to explain that her father had every intention of going with the Franks, "but their countless masses terrified him." Instead he went to Pelecanus which is close to Nicaea, where he could learn how the Franks were managing against the Turks. Alexios shrewdly planned to capture Nicaea for himself and not to receive it from the Franks, especially because not all of them had taken the oath of fealty. He sent Butumites to win the Turks inside Nicaea, which he succeeded in doing, because, Anna says, the Turks preferred to surrender to the Greeks rather than to the Franks. However, when the Turks heard that the sultan was coming to their defense, they expelled Butumites. The Latins, headed by Isangeles, arrived and started to besiege Nicaea. A fierce battle then took place between the Turks and the Latins, and the emperor sent the Franks siege engines, lights boats, heavily armed soldiers, and two thousand peltasts, with Butumites as

duke of Nicaea. Again Anna makes a point of explaining that her
father did not join the Franks as he had promised, because "no
comparison could be made between the countless hosts of the
Frankish army and his own Roman army"; also, because "he knew
the Latins' fickleness" (XI, 2, p. 272). When the Turks despaired
of the sultan's coming, they surrendered the city again to
Butumites. Anna naïvely states that Butumites cleverly arranged
the siege to make the Franks believe that he had taken the city.
Nicaea was conquered by the concerted efforts of both the
Romans and the Franks, who finally turned it back to the empire
(XI, 2, p. 273).

Alexios then asked Butumites to send the counts to Pelecanus
where he was staying with promises of "money" and "gifts,"
which, Anna repeats, was the one way Alexios could get the
Franks who had not yet taken the oath to swear fealty to the
emperor. All took the oath except Tancred, Bohemond's nephew,
who vowed fidelity to Bohemond alone, and then had the
audacity to ask for twice the "tent full of money" that Alexios
had offered to the counts before he would take the oath. It was
Bohemond who finally succeeded in getting Tancred to take the
oath.

The Franks, in company with the Roman army, took the road
to Antioch. A serious battle occurred in the plains of Dorylaeum,
and the Roman and Frankish army carried off the victory. At
Hebraïca, Bohemond descended upon Sultan Clitziasthlan "like
a lion rejoicing in his strength." They also attacked the Turks at
Augustopolis, where they routed them completely. The Latins
and the Roman army finally reached Antioch. It was here that
the rupture occurred between the Franks and the Romans.

As Anna reports it, Bohemond guilefully got Taticios and the
Roman forces to withdraw "for their own safety," then persuaded
an Armenian to open the gates to him, and thus Bohemond took
possession of Antioch. But now the Latins were shut inside since
the Turks still held the citadel and blockaded the city from the
outside. The emperor prepared to go to the assistance of the
Franks, but "a report was spread abroad that an incredible host
of barbarians was on its way to overtake him." Thus Alexios's
expedition was stopped (XI, 6, p. 283). Peter the Hermit and
his men helped the Franks. As a result of this, the Turks fled even
before the battle started. It took the Franks a whole month to
carry the Turkish booty into Antioch. The Frankish counts con-

ceded full powers over Antioch to Bohemond and set out for Jerusalem (XI, 6, 2, p. 285).

Isangeles turned over Laodicea as the emperor had ordered and marched to Tripolis, but Bohemond sent his nephew Tancred to besiege Laodicea and take it for himself. Laodicea surrendered to Tancred. When Alexios learned that Tancred had seized Laodicea, he sent Bohemond a letter asking him to withdraw from Antioch, Laodicea, and all the other cities he had taken, on the basis of the treaty made between him and the crusading chiefs. Bohemond replied that Alexios had pledged to follow them with a large army, a promise he had not kept. Alexios then sent numerous forces to subdue the whole of Cilicia, thus more easily to take Antioch. When Butumites arrived in Cilicia, he discovered that the Armenians had already concluded a truce with Tancred (XI, 9, pp. 291, 292).

At this time a Norman army arrived whose leaders were two brothers called Flanders. Like Peter the Hermit, neither did they listen to the emperor's advice to take the road the others had taken. Yet Alexios sent two of his men to accompany them in order to spare them unnecessary hardships. The Franks took Ancyra by assault and then reached a small town inhabited by the Romans. Since the citizens of this town were Christians, they did not fear the Franks. Anna writes that "the priests clad in their sacred vestments, and carrying the Gospel and crosses went out to meet their fellow Christians. But the Normans in an inhuman and merciless fashion, slaughtered not only the priests but the rest of the Christians also and then quite heedlessly continued their journey, moving in the direction of Amaseia" (X, 8, p. 289). The Turks pursued the Franks, overtook the infantry, and annihilated them completely (XI, 8, p. 290).

The Franks made a treaty with Pisa, promising large rewards for their help. Anna reports that the Pisans equipped nine hundred ships and sailed forth to meet them. Alexios sent the whole Roman fleet after them, caught up to them in Rhodes, and slaughtered the Pisan prisoners. The survivors of the Pisan fleet turned their attention to pillaging whatever islands they touched, especially Cyprus.

After the lapse of a year, Alexios was informed that the Genoese fleet was preparing to enter into alliance with the Franks. Alexios then sent Cantacuzenos with a considerable land force, and Landulph with a fleet, to engage in battle with the Genoese. When Landulph saw the large Genoese fleet, he sailed away, but the more intrepid Cantacuzenos gathered the whole fleet and pursued the Genoese. Having failed to catch them, he sailed for Laodicea to prosecute the war there with Bohemond. Cantacuzenos took possession of the harbor and town, but the citadel was still held by the Franks. When Bohemond learned of this, he united with all the forces of his nephew Tancred and Isangeles. Alexios sent a large force overland and the Romans seized the whole of Cilicia. Bohemond then entrusted Tancred with the rule of Antioch, and circulated a report that he died. Anna writes humorously that Bohemond was placed in a coffin with a cock so that it would smell like the flesh of a dead man. From Corfu, the "dead" Bohemond came to life again and sent Alexios a message that he had entrusted Antioch to Tancred; he was returning to his own country, "full of dire intentions" against Alexios, but he would return to plant his spear on Byzantium itself (XI, 12, pp. 298-99).

To counteract Bohemond's slanders against him, Alexios sent letters to Pisa, Genoa, and Venice, to warn them and prevent them from being taken in by Bohemond's lies and joining him. Bohemond maligned Alexios in Italy, Germany, and France.

Despite the hardships and humiliation Alexios endured at the hands of the crusaders, he never lost sight of the fact that they were fellow Christians. Anna shows her father's concern for the Franks when, during their crossing into Asia, the Babylonian sultan of Cairo (Caliph al-Amir) captured and imprisoned three hundred counts. Alexios sent Panucomites to the Babylonian with money and a letter in which he begged for the release of the counts. The sultan handed them over to Panucomites without taking any money. The counts were delighted over the kindness Alexios had shown them. Alexios gave them money and sent them home, not only because they wanted to leave, but to refute the tales that Bohemond was spreading about him. According to Anna, when the counts left, they "became most trustworthy evidence against Bohemond" (XII, 1, 2, pp. 301-2).

Tancred was now in Syria spreading rumors that he would soon descend on Cilicia to besiege its town and "wrest it from the Emperor's hands," since he had taken it from the Turks. Alexios left Constantinople with Empress Irene for Thessalonika, because he was suffering from gout and he needed his wife's constant care, also because of the many plots against his life which "cropped up on all sides." There Alexios prepared for Bohemond's crossing, training recruits for more than a year. When he learned that Bohemond still had not crossed, he returned to Byzantium. He sent Contostephanos to Dyrrachium to keep watch over the Straits of Lombardy to prevent Bohemond's ships from crossing when they did arrive. Contostephanos disregarded orders and crossed to Otranto, a town held by Tancred's mother. She devised schemes to keep Contostephanos in suspense, vowing loyalty to the emperor while waiting for the return of one of her sons. When her son did arrive with his fellow counts, they attacked Contostephanos and routed him completely. Several Scythians in the Roman army who had run ahead during the battle to forage were taken captive and sent to Bohemond as convincing proof that Alexios was using infidels to attack Christians. "The Pope was constrained by Bohemond's arguments," writes Anna, "and agreed with him, and sanctioned his crossing into Illyria" (XII, 8, 4, p. 318). The Franks won the first battle at Otranto, but the Romans revived it and carried off the final victory.

Bohemond returned with twelve pirate vessels and merchant ships, which Anna likens "to a floating city." For this reason she does not accuse the Constephani of cowardice for "shrinking from it in horror." Bohemond, finding free entry, crossed from Bari to Valona, disembarked his large army on the opposite coast, destroyed the whole sea coast, then proceeded to attack Dyrrachium.

Alexios now directed all his forces to reconquer the city of Antioch and rid Byzantium of Bohemond. He himself left Constantinople on November 1, 1107, Anna tells us, for Geranium, but returned four days later, because he had not seen the accustomed miracle of the Church of the Blachernae. After suitable prayers he did see the miracle, and he and the empress left again for Thessalonika, where he gathered, trained, and drilled troops from all parts of the empire. He sent letters to some of Bohemond's most intimate friends, which were supposed to be answers to letters they had sent Alexios, "wooing his friendship and revealing the tyrant's secret intentions." Alexios saw to it that these letters fell into Bohemond's hands, which made him "quite faint," Anna says, "for he believed they were true." He also sent a spy who convinced Bohemond that he was a deserter from the Roman army.

Undaunted, Bohemond poured his whole army over the plains, crossed over with an enormous fleet, and began his siege of Dyrrachium both from land and sea, with elaborate machines of battering rams, siege engines, and underground tunnels. The Roman inhabitants and the troops destroyed all these with Greek fire, which they poured on the Franks. They also blocked him by land and sea, so that all supplies were cut off. Bohemond finally sent envoys to Alexios and began to sue for peace, which the emperor judged it wise to accept. After exchanging hostages, and after Bohemond himself met the envoys sent by Alexios, the Frank agreed to be "faithful liegeman" to Alexios and John Porphyrogenitos. In the ten-page treaty recorded by Anna in its entirety, Bohemond agreed to hold Antioch during his lifetime, then revert it back to the empire. He also agreed that the patriarch of Antioch was to be a Greek (XIII, 12, p. 354).

Bohemond suddenly abandoned his troops and returned to his wife and two daughters. According to Anna, he died in 1108. Chalandon states that he died in 1111.[47] Tancred retained the principality of Antioch until December 12, 1112.

Anna's Hellenic eyewitness report of the First Crusade is extremely important for several reasons. It is true, as Krumbacher states, that in her "interpretation of the Crusades, Anna is understandably a Byzantine woman."[48] Yet her report served to expose the myth long held by Western civilization that the Frankish counts were chiefly inspired by religious motives. We also learn from her colorful battle scenes between the Franks and the Greeks the Latin methods of warfare, the crossbow, a weapon unknown to the Greeks, and their strategically planned campaigns against her father, which Anna praises with unusual objectivity. "Anna Comnena describes in bold strokes the military prowess of the Normans and Latins," writes Vryonis, "filling out her story with detailed observations on Latin superiority in military technology."[49] She includes one siege, the siege of Castoria, concerning which she is our only source.[50]

Anna's errors in the case of the First Crusade are largely those of omission. In her filial endeavor to give an emphatic report of her father's struggle with the recalcitrant Frankish counts, especially with Bohemond whose bad faith caused Alexios so much vexation, she does not present with complete objectivity the gains that Alexios made with the help of the crusaders. Oman states that with the help of the crusaders Alexios regained possession of Nicaea, recovered all of Lydia and Caria, and much of Phrygia. Alexios was free of the danger of the Muslims of Asia Minor and Syria; between 1100 and the year of his death in 1118, Alexios was able to strengthen his position at home and abroad.[51]

Buckler notes other omissions and inaccuracies in Anna's report of the First Crusade. She points out that Anna says nothing of Bohemond's captivity (1100-1103).[52] Anna's account of the crusade after Taticios left Antioch is meager and inaccurate. She says that Godfrey of Bouillon was captured by the Turks at the battle of Rama, which actually took place after his death.[53]

Alexios sought to use the crusaders as mercenaries to recover the regions he had lost. The Latins complained that he did not follow the crusaders with an army as he had promised. Anna admits this and gives the reasons, though not very convincingly. It is also true, however, that the Frankish counts wanted to carve out principalities for themselves. All the trouble began when Bohemond refused to restore Antioch to the emperor as he had promised. Bohemond was the only crusader with whom Alexios broke off friendly relations. It is generally admitted that he retained friendly relations with all the other counts.

V   *The War of Alexios Against Heresy*

For he had studied the Holy Writings more than anybody else in order to sharpen his tongue for wrestlings with the heretics . . . I for my part should call him "the thirteenth apostle." (XIV, 8, p. 386)

It is obvious, from all that Anna writes, that Alexios, "the faithful in Christ, Emperor of the Romans," not only encouraged scholars to study the divine writings rather than Greek literature, but that as the chief protector of Orthodoxy, he gave priority to his religious functions over all other matters of state. Anna does not exaggerate when she calls her father "the thirteenth apostle." The twelfth-century historians noted, as Oeconomos observes, that "the Comneni Emperors were more eager than the patriarchs or the high dignitaries of the Church to take in their hands the defense of orthodoxy."[54] But what is even more revealing about their passionate zeal for Orthodoxy, is "that the Church not only combatted heresy and superstition, but it tried to deroot from Byzantine soil new ideas contrary to its dogma."[55]

To the Byzantine, Hellenization and Orthodoxy were one. Hence, it is not surprising that Anna, who was as dedicated to

Orthodoxy as her father, should give such wide coverage to the heretical disturbances in her father's reign. She saw all heretics as spoilers of the faith, which she regarded as the extreme expression established by God, in Christian values and in the Greek language. Religious dissent, for her, took dangerous forms and was counter to the will of God. Nonetheless, it is as Hussey asserts, that in the ecclesiastical sphere, tradition largely determined the actions of Alexios. Anna felt no different.

Anna writes of Philippopolis, whose chief misfortune, she thinks, was the residence of so many heretics there: Armenians, Bogomils, "and even those most godless Paulicians" (XIV, 8, p. 384). Her father had made an attempt to transplant the Paulicians to Thrace, as she explains, "firstly to drive them out of their strong cities and forts which they held as despotic rulers, and secondly to post them as trustworthy guards against the inroads of the Scythians by which the country was often oppressed" (XIV, 8, 4, p. 385).

Anna offers the reader no reasons for the enmity of the Paulicians who, as Charanis observes, cooperated with the enemy whenever the opportunity presented itself. One example which he gives is the cooperation of the Bogomils in 1086, when they urged the Pechenegs and Cumans to invade the Empire, an invasion repeated several times, which devastated Thrace and came close to overwhelming the Byzantine capital. The energy and diplomacy of Alexios I Comnenos saved the situation.[56]

The first trial which Anna discusses caused her father considerable vexation since it had to do with his appropriation of the church vessels which he had turned into coin to continue the war against the Normans and the Turks. She naturally defends her father's stand against Leo, metropolitan of Chalcedon, chief objector of the Synod, since the more distinguished members of the Synod were with her father on this.

As Anna reports this trial, Leo had laid down the principle that sacred images should be adored and not only given relative honor (V, 2, p. 119). As Hussey explains this, "Leo was accused by a Synod of worshipping icons *latreftikos,* whereas they could only be reverenced *schetikos";* that is to say, the material of which they were made ceased to have any special value once it was melted down and no longer represented any special figure.[57] Her father exhorted Leo "to change his opinion about the images," but Leo, who "attacked the Emperor most impudently" despite

Alexios's promises "to restore even finer vessels to the churches and do all that was necessary to repair the loss," was deposed from office (V, 2, 1, p. 119). The report of the Synod states that Leo repented wholeheartedly.[58] Anna says that Leo continued to disturb the church, which resulted in a sentence of exile to the city of Sozopolis on the Black Sea, where he was treated "with much care and consideration by order of the Emperor" (V, 2, p. 119).

Anna's report on the trial of Italos, the popular Italian-born philosopher, differs markedly from the existing "Report of the Trial" and the *Synodicon*: there are differences concerning the date, the accusation, and the trial itself.

She states that the trial of Italos took place in 1084; she recalls that her father was anxious to march against the Frank Bryennios who had taken Castoria, but he deferred the expedition to attend to the trial of Italos (V, 8, p. 132). Chalandon states that the taking of Castoria occurred in October or November, 1083, for Alexios reentered Constantinople on the first of December.[59] The "Report of the Trial" published by Th. Uspensky in the *Bulletin de l'Institut archaeologique russe de Constantinople*, Vol. II (1897), gives the date as Indiction V, which occurs from September 1, 1081 through August 31, 1082.[60]

Anna's six-page report of this trial of Italos gives us a prejudiced portrait of a brilliant Neo-platonic philosopher using bad manners and bad grammar. In her estimation, Italos was clever and had a quick intelligence because of "his mother's ardent supplications"; she admits that Italos was thoroughly acquainted with Greek and Chaldaean literature; he was well versed in dialectics and in the rules of Aristotle; she also admits that youth flocked to his lectures. What she highlights, possibly because of his extraordinary popularity, is his ugly appearance, his barbarous disposition, his abhorrent grammar, and his unpolished language. She tells us that he lacked refinement and had a violent temper which was followed by tears and evident remorse. As for his teaching. Italos gave instruction in philosophy as a "serviceable tool" (V, 9, p. 135). The *Synodicon* deprecates the ecclesiastical doctrine.[61] Nicetas Chionates states that Italos exercised great influence on the men of his time, occupying the highest functions at court.[62] What is astonishing is Anna's condemnation of Italos, when he was the disciple and successor of Psellos, the man for whom she had the greatest admiration.[63]

As for the trial itself, what we learn from Anna is that her father deputized his brother Isaac the Sebastocrator to examine him; he censured him publicly, and passed him on to the ecclesiastical tribunal by order of the emperor. When Italos continued "to act like a buffoon" the president of the Tribunal, Eustratios Garidas, condemned him to detention, but then Anna reveals that Italos won Garidas over to his side, whereupon the whole population of Constantinople surged into Hagia Sophia shouting for Italos, (V, 9, 1, p. 136). Anna charges Italos with his belief in metempsychosis, his Platonic and Neo-platonic doctrines, and his insulting words about the holy icons of the saints. She does not specify on the heretical points on which Italos was accused; she does say that his heretical doctrines were summarized in eleven sections and sent to the, emperor, who made Italos recite them from the pulpit of Hagia Sophia, with his head uncovered, and pronounce a curse upon them while the whole congregation listened and repeated the curse. Italos continued to teach his doctrines, however, and he was excommunicated. Subsequently, he professed penitence and his sentence was lightened somewhat (V, 8, 9, pp. 132-37).

Both the "Report of the Trial" and the *Synodicon* contain the heretical points for which Italos was accused; they were publicly anathematized on the first Sunday in Lent.[64] It appears that Italos's orthodoxy had been questioned in 1077 during the reign of Michael VII Ducas, but because of the friendship of the emperor it had gone no further. Early in January 1082, Alexios received an anonymous letter (the author of which later turned out to be one Michael Caspax), which accused Italos of professing heretical opinions contrary to the Holy Scriptures and the traditions of the church. Italos appeared before a council and presented his profession of faith, but Patriarch Eustratios Garidas, who presided, turned the case over to Alexios because of the clamors of the crowd, or probably because at the start Garidas spoke of Italos in favorable terms. Alexios formed another commission composed of the delegates of the patriarch and the Senate before which Italos read a statement of his doctrines. The commission made no decision; instead they presented their findings to the emperor. Alexios sent Italos again before the Patriarch and the Council; but without waiting for their decision, he pronounced the anathema against Italos, who was excommunicated on March 13.[65]

Hussey, who has made a careful study of both the *Synodicon* and the "Report of the Trial," states that the six theological points upon which Italos was found heretical do not correspond either with Anna's account or with the eleven counts specified in the *Synodicon*. She also notes that the *Synodicon* inaccurately accuses Italos of denying the immortality of the soul and resurrection, while affirming the eternity of the world. Hussey thinks that Italos's continued teaching of his doctrines may imply a second trial; but there are no details of this. The only thing that can be said with certainty, Hussey concludes, is that Italos was interested in philosophy and that he was a Neo-platonist, as revealed in his published writings.[66]

What becomes clear from all this is that Italos appears quite different from the man whom Anna depicts in her *Alexiad*. According to Chalandon, Italos "recognized his errors on certain points, discussed others and affirmed with dignity what he believed to be healthy and just."[67]

Anna's next report is on the monk Nilos and his Armenian followers and Blachernites, an ordained priest. While she admits that Nilos "had studied the writings of the saints very closely," and that he had a large "far from ignoble body of followers," partly because of his austere morals, she indicts him because he knew nothing of the "Church's teaching of the 'hypostatical union'" and of the two natures in Christ; that is to say, how the assumption of human nature was made divine. Nilos, according to Anna, foolishly thought that nature had made it divine (X, 1, p. 235). Alexios held a public Synod attended by the whole body of the higher clergy and by Patriarch Nicolas III, known as the Grammarian. The Synod laid Nilos under permanent anathema. Blachernites, an ordained priest, whom Anna associates with the Monophysite heretics, widespread during her father's reign, and the Bogomils, was also tried for holding tenets foreign to the church's teachings. Alexios instructed him, but since he would not abandon his beliefs, he too was condemned to permanent anathema.

Her last report on the heretics is on Basil, head of the Bogomils, whom Anna associates with Manichaeism, the Paulician heresy, and the "shamelessness of the Massalians." She charges the Bogomils with heretical views as to Christ's two natures, the Incarnation, calling the church "temples of devils," and his disbelief in transubstantiation. She takes pleasure in recalling

how her father brought the Bogomils to the light "by chanting
mysterious spells" (XX, 8, p. 412-13). She is awestruck once more
as she recalls a miracle of stones thrown at Basil's cell, probably
as a "burst of anger of Satanael's attendant demons," but she
refuses to expound the whole heresy of the Bogomils because
"modesty prevents her"; instead she refers the reader to *Dogmatic
Panoply,* a book which her father commissioned the monk
Euthymios Zygabenos to write (XV, 9, 415). Basil was trapped
into giving an account of his teaching and professing his doctrine; Alexios and his brother Isaac pretended that they were
anxious to join his sect for the salvation of their souls; then, Anna
tells us, Alexios drew back a curtain and revealed in the next
room the Senate, soldiers, and ecclesiastics waiting with the patriarch to condemn the unfortunate Bogomil. Basil, according
to Anna, "showed himself contemptuous of all punishments and
threats" and was burned alive at the Hippodrome (XV, 10,
p. 417).

In no other section of the *Alexiad* is Anna so completely dominated by the Byzantine fanatic zeal for orthodox dogma as she
is in her report of these four heretic trials. Nowhere else does
she appear to be less of an objective historian. What comes
through from her report is the general weakness of the church.

CHAPTER 7

Anna Comnena, Historian

I Her Contribution to History

The *Alexiad* is the first great work of the Hellenic Renaissance which starts with the Comneni and ends with the Palaeologi. (Karl Krumbacher, *Geschichte der Byzantinischen Litteratur*, Munich, 1897, p. 270)

ANNA'S Hellenic account of her father's reign is an invaluable historical document despite her instances of unhistorical partiality. From the first edition which crawled out of obscurity five centuries after it was written, the *Alexiad* has been gaining recognition, until now it has come full circle to fill a gap in Byzantine history and correct a distorted perspective of the history of Byzantium, created chiefly by Gibbons's *Decline and Fall* and by Sir Walter Scott's ridiculous portrayal of Anna in his *Count Robert of Paris.*

Probably Anna's most important contribution to history is her account of the First Crusade, for the reasons already stated. Invaluable for the student of Byzantine history is Anna's detailed account of the Turkish incursions on Byzantium, especially those of the Patzinaks. for which Anna is our only source.[1] Chalandon notes that the greater part of the events which occurred in Asia Minor are known to us only through the *Alexiad.*[2] Her dramatic description of the Muslim raids convey to the reader the perils that beset her father from the very outset of his reign as Seljuks, Patzinaks, Uzes, and other Turkish tribes, threatened not only the frontiers of the empire but the very walls of Constantinople. Anna knew the mentality of the Turks; she was familiar with their character as a people; she writes of their domestic quarrels, their rivalries, their methods of warfare which her father understood so well that he could advise the crusaders how to do battle with them. Indeed, it was his understanding, his close association with the Turks, his ability to maneuver with them when he needed them as allies, and when they fought against him, that

149

lengthened the life of Byzantium and helped to preserve the
heritage of the Greeks for another three centuries. "The happy
results of his reign will follow him under his son John . . ." writes
Chalandon.[3]

Under Alexios's strategic and diplomatic leadership, the frontiers of Byzantium were extended both in Europe and in Asia.
"After thirty-seven arduous years as ruler, Alexios had greatly
strengthened the Empire and restored its glory," writes Vryonis,
"having found Byzantium virtually destroyed, deprived of its
fairest provinces, and with the foes at the door. Through sheer
ability, he defeated the Normans, destroyed the Patzinaks,
exploited the Crusaders and forced the Turks to retreat."[4]

In Anna's portrayal of life at the Byzantine court in which
she grew up and resided until the death of her father, we have
a first-hand report of the court intrigues of the imperial family,
as well as their fierce solidarity in support of their vested interests; the rivalries, the diplomatic moves, and the rebellions of
several members of the feudal aristocracy, each vying for power
and seizure of the Byzantine throne. The *Alexiad* presents lively
pen portraits not only of the subject of her history and her mother
Empress Irene but also of her uncle Isaac; the Mother of the
Comneni; her uncle George Palaeologos; and even of the enemy
Bohemond, the Frankish count for whom, according to some
Byzantine historians, Anna felt a sinister attraction. We get to
know their way of life at the court, their morals, their ideals
of learning, as well as her own, the religious climate of her
father's reign, the heresies of the time. Anna's report of her
imperial life as a princess in a feudal society is a primary source
for her age, written by a woman well qualified as a distinguished,
cultured, and educated member of the military aristocracy of
the Byzantine court. But "almost as far down as the nineteenth
century a woman as an historian was indeed a *rara avis*," writes
one critic, "when therefore a princess arose in one of the most
momentous movements in human history she surely deserves the
respectful attention of posterity."[5]

The authentic documents that Anna records verbatim are
particularly valuable. The first Golden Bull she records in her
history is the one her father issued entrusting her grandmother
Anna Dalassena with the single-handed running of the imperial
government when he was forced to be away from the capital
(III, 6, pp. 83-84). In the same book Anna also records one of

the letters Alexios wrote to the king of Germany in which he tries to bring about an alliance of marriage between his brother's son John and the daughter of the king of Germany in an attempt to join him in the war he was waging against Robert Guiscard (III, 10, pp. 91-93). In Book VIII, Anna gives us two letters written by her father after he learned from the archbishop of Bulgaria that his nephew John, Duke of Dyrrachium and the Sebastocrator's son, was accused of rebellion. One of these letters he addressed to John himself asking for his presence; the other letter was addressed to leading men of Dyrrachium to arrest John if he proved recalcitrant or refused to obey (VIII, 7, pp. 208-9). Anna records the letters exchanged between Bohemond and her father concerning the oaths and promises he and the Frankish counts had taken, and which they had broken; the letter in which Bohemond blames the emperor for breaking his promise to follow the crusaders with a large army is also included (XI, 8, pp. 290-91). In Book XIII, Anna gives the reader the longest document between Bohemond and her father, written in 1109, invalidating their first agreement because he had declared war against Alexios and stipulating the terms in detail of the new Golden Bull officially signed in red ink (XIII, 12, pp. 348-58).

One Chrysobull issued by Alexios which Anna does not include is a serious omission. This is the one entitled "Guildsmen and Merchants may not take the oath in their homes." Vryonis, who brings this to our attention, is not certain of the date of this decree, but he notes that it was pronounced in a dispute over certain merchandise between two merchants and a woman named Anna. "When the former were asked to testify under oath," writes Vryonis, "they demanded to take the oath in their homes rather than in a public court, claiming this prerogative on the grounds that they were both senators."[6] This Chrysobull reveals the democratization process which was going on in the reign of Alexios, despite the feudalization of the empire. Obviously, Anna was not interested in the democratization of the Byzantine Empire.

Anna says nothing about her father as a writer, which would have added a new dimension to Alexios not only as a ruler but as a father and as a man. There are extant twenty-four imperial novels and golden bulls written by Alexios, five of which, according to Buckler, deal with female rights and duties.[7] Also extant are two poems to his son John, the first of which consists of four hundred and twenty lines, and the second, an unfinished poem which consists of eighty-one lines. There is still another poem of one hundred iambic twelve-syllable lines headed "Prayer of the Emperor Alexios," which is contained in a manuscript at the Bodleian Library.[8] Alexios wrote several theological treatises against heretics. His *Muses,* written a short time before his death, were published in 1913. They were written in iambic meter in the form of an "exhortation" and dedicated to John. "These *Muses,*" writes Vasiliev, "were a kind of political will, concerned not only with abstract problems of morality, but also with many contemporary historical events, such as the First Crusade."[9]

Her greatest contribution to history, of course, is her three-dimensional portrait of her father as a monarch and as a military strategist. It is a panegyric of Alexios, inspired by Homer's epic, yet it is also a realistic portrayal of a monarch who was beset by enemies both domestic and foreign. Despite his ruses and dissimulations, Alexios was also a man blessed with a sense of *philanthropia.* His most significant contribution in this direction is his Orphanage about which Anna writes fully and without exaggeration; other contemporary Byzantine historians also have praised Alexios for the Orphanage. Zonaras writes that Alexios had renovated the Orphanage and placed in it numerous old people in need of care; furthermore, he built within it residences for nuns and monks and a school for orphans or poor children. He placed teachers, educators, and provisions for all of them.[10]

Modern Byzantine historians also recognize the greatness of Alexios. "He was a man of talent," writes Chalandon; "he stopped for a time the slow disintegration of the diverse elements of which the Empire was formed."[11] And Krumbacher states, "In spite of all defects these memoirs of the daughter about the father remain as one of the most eminent works of medieval Greek historiography."[12] Indeed, one might add without exaggeration, that Anna's status in Byzantine historiography has now extended beyond the borders of Byzantium. There is no comparable work by any woman Eastern or Western. On the whole, her *Alexiad* is objectively conceived and objectively executed.

II *Evaluation*

The *Alexiad* of Anna Comnena, daughter of Alexios, is without doubt the most remarkable of the works of Byzantine historiography, not only as a historic source of her father's reign, but clearly for its literary worth. (Radoslav Katičič, "Anna i Komnene, Kai O omeros," *Epeteris Etairias Byzantinon Spoudon*, Vol. 27 [Athens, 1957], p. 213)

As Anna has repeatedly informed the reader in several sections of her history, she derived part of her history from her own memory, part from the men who had been soldiers when her father ascended the throne, and who accompanied the emperor on his campaigns. These she valued because they were "simple in diction, incurious and strictly truthful and displayed no style and were free of all rhetorical pretensions" (XIV, 7, 3, p. 382). She also tells the reader that she gathered part of her material during the reign of her nephew Manuel, son of John II, "when all flatteries and lies about his grandfather had expired together" (XIV, 7, 3, p. 381).

Anna naturally learned the facts of her early childhood from her parents and older relatives closest to her. When she was old enough to accompany her parents on their expeditions, she herself was an eyewitness to the events that took place. As has already been stated, aside from oral sources, she also used written sources, as state archives, diplomatic correspondence, and imperial decrees. There were also enough people still living during the years when she was writing her *Alexiad* who had known her father and informed her of his doings. By all standards of historiography, then, it can safely be said that the *Alexiad* is a primary source of her father's reign.

Anna's account reflects the prevailing standards of her age and of her class. She was infinitely more cultured than most of her father's aristocratic subjects; she was certainly the most enlightened woman of her age. She would naturally be inured to use the cultural and Christian rationale of her class. Her point of view is feudal, military; it represents the slave-owning aristocracy and the wealthy landowning class of Asia Minor to which both her parents and the Bryenni family belonged. The reader will find no mention in Anna's history of the condition of the common people, or the social unrest and the political uprisings which occurred during her father's reign. She seems to have no interest whatever in the other classes of Byzantium. Anna's account of her father's reign is palace oriented, woven out of the fabric of her training and her environment.

In part, her approach was influenced by the Greek historians

Herodotos, Thucydides, and Polybios, whose work she knew well. Herodotos wrote his *History* in order that the deeds of men might not be effaced by time nor remain unsung, which Anna states as her own purpose in her Preface (I, 1, p. 1). Thucydides wrote of causes and events that he either saw himself or heard from the testimony of others, which he carefully examined. This Anna does with meticulous honesty. Polybios felt it his greatest duty as a historian to be impartial, which is Anna's sincere intention as she repeatedly avows.

But Anna's approach to history is also a blend of the Byzantine view of religion. If the Byzantine view of religion was one of Providential design, then Anna leans more heavily on that side, for the predominant tone of the *Alexiad* is a religious one. Providence appears in almost every page of her history. In essence, however, her approach to history is most significantly identified with what has come to be known as the "cult of personality." For Anna, the destiny of Byzantium was shaped chiefly by the force of one great man: her father Alexios I, emperor of the Romans, who was destined by Providence to restore Byzantium.

Anna's method was one of simple comparison. As she herself tells us, she compared the accounts of the old men, what they had told her, what she remembered from often having heard the accounts both from her father and from her paternal and maternal uncles, and what she herself had witnessed. From all these sources, she says, she wove the whole fabric of her truthful history (XIV, 7, 3, p. 382).

As has been stated elsewhere, one of her sources to which she refers the reader on five different occasions is her husband's unfinished history *Hyle Historias*, which she claims is fuller than her own. The *Hyle* ends in 1079 because of the untimely death of Bryennios. In her Preface, she erroneously states that her husband's history begins with the reign of Romanos IV Diogenes instead of the reign of Emperor Isaac Comnenos, first of the Comneni dynasty to rule Byzantium. Buckler has noted that the opening of the second chapter of her first book is almost a paraphrase of Book II, Chapter 21 of the *Hyle,* and even more closely copied are the three speeches put into her father's mouth in the same episode. Her report of the rebels Bryennios and Basilacios are found in Book IV of her husband's history.[13]

For Byzantine events before her father's lifetime, Anna referred to the *Chronographia* of Michael Psellos, "prince of philosophers."

The *Chronographia* covers a period of one hundred years, beginning with the accession of Basil II (976) and ending with the accession of Nicephoros Botaneiates (1077). She also used the Byzantine chronicler and theologian Joannes Zonaras, who lived in Constantinople where he served as commander of the Imperial Guard and was private secretary to Alexios I. His work *Epitomi Historiai* (a compendium of history in eighteen books) extends from the creation to the death of Alexios in 1118. Anna also used the *Synopsis Istorion* of Joannes Scylitzes, a history of the Eastern Roman Empire covering the years 811 to 1057. The *Historia* of Michael Attaleiates (1079-80), which covers the period 1034-79, is another of her sources. For her reports on the heretical trials she referred to Euthymios Zigabenos's *Dogmatic Panoply*, which she advises us to read for a fuller knowledge of these reports.

One cannot omit from this evaluation of Anna's history her filial devotion, which understandably colors her history, despite her often-repeated avowals to write an account of her father's reign based strictly on historical facts. As Diehl has asserted, "the *Alexiad* is less the title of a history book than the title of an epic poem, written to celebrate a legendary hero."[14] This is not to say that Anna makes no sincere effort to be impartial about her father's deeds; indeed, considering the three decades which transpired between his death and her writing of the *Alexiad*, she recounts facts with unusual objectivity and accuracy. She has been seriously criticized for omitting all mention of the role she and her mother played during those last moments in her father's life, although one can understand the reason. There is a wide discrepancy between what she writes of these last hours in the life of her father and the report of Nicetas Chionates already noted. On the whole, however, the *Alexiad* is an honest appraisal of her father's reign and a frank statement of her own Byzantine beliefs.

A word must be added about Anna as a writer. In the main, the *Alexiad* is written in Attic Greek. Basically, our porphyrogenete adheres to classic tradition and form. She herself has informed us that she carried her study of Greek to the highest pitch" (Preface, P. 1). Zonaras states that she had "a precisely atticizing language."[15] In other words, Anna made an attempt to imitate the Attic, and in large part it is accurate Attic. As Antoniades states, Anna was proud of her eclectic training and she was therefore, not so much concerned about reflecting the language of her epoch, as she was of reflecting the Homeric, Platonic, and Thucydidean language which she used with great facility.[16] Thucydides influenced her most; it must be added, however, that her style of writing was also influenced by two Byzantine writers: Ioannes Epiphaneus and Theophylaktos Simokattes.[17] Haritonides states that her language is archaic but not without a mixture of the spoken language of the day.[18]

One cannot possibly identify all of Anna's unclassical deviations in a few pages. Buckler, who has probably made the most detailed analysis of Anna's writings, divides Anna's unclassical words and words unclassically used in three categories: non-Latin, old Latin, and medieval, but concludes that there are few non-Latin and medieval words in the *Alexiad*.[19]

Most numerous are Anna's old Latin words, which had long been assimilated into the Greek language. On four random pages of Book XI of the *Alexiad* (Leib III, pp. 7, 8, 11, 12), I found *komites* (counts); *courtins* (curtains); *komitouras* (companies); *Frangikou fossaton* (Frankish boundary) from the Latin *Fussatum* meaning boundary; *kastellion* (castle from the Latin *castellum*).

Anna's abundant use of old words with new meanings may be logically traced to the *koine*, the language which was used in Greece from 323 B.C. to 330 A.D. The *koine* identified with the New Testament became the standard in Byzantine learning and writing. Living in a Christian epoch, profoundly indoctrinated in the Orthodox faith, Anna would naturally use the meanings of words found in the *koine*. As Anna uses the word *ecclesia*, it means church, not the classical assembly; *litourgia* means liturgy, not public service to the state; *episcopos* in Byzantine as well as modern Greek means a bishop, not an overseer; *monachos* in Attic means alone; in modern Greek it means alone and monk; as Anna used the word it means a monk. In the Attic, *diabolos* meant a slanderer; as Anna uses the word it means a devil.

What makes the *Alexiad* so difficult to read are the grammatical deviations from the classic, only a few of which can be considered here. In the post-classical epoch, a whole list of nouns took the neuter gender and the ending *ion*. For example, Anna uses the neuter *kaukion* (chalice) instead of the classical masculine *kaukos;* the neuter *margaritarion* (pearl) replaces masculine *margaritis* (Leib I, p. 135). Antoniades notes that these words refer to the gifts that Alexios sent the king of Alamania, which are the "bibelots" of a Christian period, and Anna cannot help but use them as they are heard in their daily lives.[20] In the word *mosuna* (wooden tower) (Leib III, p. 9), Anna uses the neuter instead of the classical masculine; she uses the Latin word *bukina* (from the Latin *bucina* meaning trumpet) as a neuter noun instead of the classical form of the masculine or feminine (Leib III, p. 12).

There are syntactical deviations from the Attic. For example, the word *ephevron* (discovered), a second aorist in the classical language appears as *ephevrosan,* which is a first aorist (Leib III, p. 192). Both Antoniades and Buckler agree that as Anna uses the word *sozousan,* which is the present participle feminine accusative singular in the classical, and meant *saving,* it is nearer to the modern Greek *sonei* meaning it is enough.[21] Anna writes of the Roman army not being equal *sozousan* even to a small part of the barbarian forces (Leib II, p. 88). She speaks of her father's troops amounting only to a small part of Robert's forces *dynameis mede to polloston ton tou Rombertou sozousas* (saving not even a fraction of Robert's forces) (Leib I, p. 146). And again, she writes of forces which were equal to only a minimal part of the forces which were there, *mede to polloston tes epi-katalambanouses dynameos sozontas* (saving not even the smallest fraction of the occupying power (Leib II, p. 79). Anna uses the phrase *kai tas sozousas apololekotas elpidas,* which Leib translates as having lost all saving hope (Leib II, p. 143).

These are only a few of the deviations that are found in the *Alexiad* which make it extremely difficult to read. For this reason, probably more than any other, Anna's "purist" style of writing has been severely criticized. Krumbacher implies that Anna Comnena used the mummified language found in the writings of her age.[22] This was probably best explained by Dawkins, who classifies it as a mixture of the classic forms of the written tradition as part of the ordinary spoken Greek of the day. The *koine* standardized the Greek language, but "it inevitably produced a certain deadness, as learning and literature became the close preserve of trained scholars rather than a field open to all comers."[23]

What should not be overlooked, it seems to me, for a fair appraisal of Anna both as a historiographer and as a writer, is that she is the first and only woman who wrote history in Byzantium.

N. Iorga feels that "taken as a whole, the *Alexiad* is the very tableau of the Byzantine Empire under Alexios I and Anna without doubt has fulfilled the difficult task she assigned to herself."[24] Anna achieved her purpose in her portrayal of her father as a Byzantine emperor whose military strategy extended the survival of the Hellenic heritage for at least three centuries.

Notes and References

List of abbreviations
B. Z. = *Byzantinische Zeitschrift*
n   = note
P. G. = (Migne's) *Patrologia Graeca*. Vols. 127, 133.

Preface

1. Sternbach, I Appendix III Rosprawy Akad. Umiejet, wydzial filol. (Krakow). Ser. II, XXI, 1903, p. 360, apud Georgina Buckler, *Anna Comnena* (Oxford, 1968), p. 6 and n. 1.
2. Gustave Schlumberger, *Revue des Etudes Grecques*, VII (1894), p. 331, no. 129.
3. Ed. Kurtz, "Prologos eis tin diataxin tis Kaisarissis Kyras Annis os par ekeinis ekdothis," "Unedierte texte aus der Zeit des Kaisers Johannes Komnenus," in *B. Z.* XVI (Leipzig, 1907), pp. 98-101.
4. Joh. Conradi Fueslini, *Dissertatio de Alexiade Annae Comnenae* (Thuringia, 1766), p. 16.
5. *Ibid.*, and Bernard Leib, "Contribution à l'étude des manuscrits et du texte de l'*Alexiade* d'Anne Comnène," in *Mélanges Charles Diehl*, Vol. I (Paris, 1930), p. 191.
6. Fueslini, *op. cit.*, p. 14.
7. *Ibid.*
8. Diehl, *op. cit.*, p. 192.
9. Fueslini, *op. cit.*, p. 14.
10. Diehl, *op. cit.*, p. 194.

Chronology

1. Anne Comnena states that her mother "had not completed her fifteenth year," in 1081, which puts her birthdate at 1066, *Alexiad*, III, 3, p. 77.
2. "Porphyrogenete," born in the purple room; that is to say, born to royalty (VII, 2, p. 170).
3. Theophylactos speaks of Isaac's death in one of his letters (pp. 12, 377 ff.), which places his death before 1108; apud F. Chalandon, *Essai sur le régne d'Alexis Ier Comnène, 1081-1118* (Paris 1900), p. 273, n. 2.
4. The death of Irene is fixed by the mention in the *Typikon* of the Kosmosoteira, as the 19th of February of the First Indiction.

The *Typikon* of the Pantocrator of John II in 1136 tells us that his mother was already deceased. Chalandon thinks the closest date for the death of Irene is 1133, apud Jean Darrouzès, *Georges et Demetrios Tornikes, Lettres et Discours* (Paris, 1970), pp. 304-5, n. 90.

5. Although the exact date of Anna's death is unknown, the "Discourse on the Death of the Porphyrogenete Kyra Anna the Kaisarissa," by Georgios Tornikes, delivered at the end of 1154 or the beginning of 1155, would indicate that Anna was deceased before that year.

Chapter One

1. Joan Hussey, "The Later Macedonians, the Comneni, and the Angelis, 1025-1204," in *Cambridge Medieval History*, IV, Part 1, p. 194 (2nd. ed.).

2. George Ostrogorsky, "Table of Maps" (second map), in *History of the Byzantine State*, translated by Joan Hussey (New Brunswick, New Jersey, 1957).

3. Charles Diehl, *History of the Byzantine Empire* (New York, 1967), pp. 77, 84, 95.

4. Ostrogorsky, *op. cit.*, p. 295.

5. *Ibid.*

6. Peter Charanis, "The Byzantine Empire in the Eleventh Century," p. 182, in *A History of the Crusades*, ed. K. M. Setton (Philadelphia, 1955), Vol. I, pp. 177-219.

7. Ostrogorsky, *op. cit.*, p. 303.

8. Frederick Chalandon, *Histoire de la Domination Normande en Italie et en Sicile* (Paris, 1907), Vol. I, p. 48.

9. Charanis, *op cit.*, p. 203.

10. Ostrogorsky, *op. cit.*, p. 291.

11. Diehl, *op. cit.*, p. 100.

12. Steven Runciman, *The History of the Crusades* (Cambridge, 1957), Vol. I, p. 68.

13. S. Khuda Bukhsh, *Contributions to the History of Islamic Civilization* (Calcutta, 1905), p. 204.

14. Claude Cahen, "The Turkish Invasion: The Selchukids," p. 136, in *A History of the Crusades*, ed. K. M. Setton, Vol. I (Madison, Wisconsin, 1969), second edition, pp. 135-76.

15. J. Kordatos, *Istoria tis Byzantinis Autokratorias* (Athens, 1959), Vol. I, p. 501.

16. Khuda Bukhsh, *op. cit.*, p. 200.

17. Michael Psellos, "Constantine VIII," in *Fourteen Byzantine Rulers*, the *Chronographia*, translated by E. R. A. Sewter (London, 1966), p. 53.

18. "Byzantion" in *Megale Helleniki Engyklopaidia*, second edition, ed. Pavlos Drandaki (Athens), Vol. 7, p. 863.

19. Chalandon, *op. cit.*, p. 73.
20. *Ibid.*, p. 89.
21. Claude Cahen, *Pre-Ottoman Turkey*, translated from the French by J. Jones-Williams (London, 1968), p. 68.
22. Hussey, *op. cit.*, p. 197.
23. Psellos, "Zoe and Theodora," *op. cit.*, p. 158.
24. *Ibid.*, "Constantine IX," p. 170.
25. *Ibid.*, pp. 250-51.
26. Cecaumenos, "Strategicon," Ch. 50, apud Joan Hussey, *op. cit.*, p. 204.
27. Ostrogorsky, *op. cit.*, p. 329.
28. *Ibid.*, p. 330.
29. *Ibid.*, pp. 292-93.
30. Hussey, *op. cit.*, p. 202.
31. Charanis, *op. cit.*, p. 185.
32. *Ibid.*
33. Diehl, *op. cit.*, pp. 107-9.
34. Cahen, *op. cit.*, p. 70.
35. Psellos, "Michael VI," *op. cit.*, pp. 276, 277, 278.
36. Charanis, *op. cit.*, pp. 190-91.
37. *Ibid.*, p. 185.
38. Nicephoros Bryennios, *Hyle Historias*, translated into French under the title "Les Quatres Livres des Histoires," by Henri Grégoire, in *Byzantion* 23 (1953), Book I, 4, p. 478.
39. Sir Charles Oman, *Story of the Byzantine Empire* (London, 1892), p. 250.
40. Psellos, "Constantine X," *op. cit.*, p. 339.
41. Eugen Stanescu, "Les contre-réformes de Constantine Ducas," in *Proceedings of the XIIIth International Congress of Byzantine Studies*, Oxford 5-10 September 1966 (London, 1967), p. 405.
42. Robert S. Lopez, "The Norman Conquest of Sicily," p. 59, in *A History of the Crusades*, ed. K. M. Setton (Philadelphia, 1955), pp. 54-67.
43. Hussey, *op. cit.*, p. 208.
44. Psellos, *op. cit.*, p. 232, n. 2.
45. Hussey, *op. cit.*, p. 209.
46. Charanis, *op. cit.*, p. 191.
47. Speros Vryonis, Jr., "Byzantine *Demokratia* and the Guilds in the 11th Century," in *Dumbarton Oaks Papers*, No. 17 (Washington, 1963), p. 309 and references.
48. Psellos, *op. cit.*, p. 338.
49. *Ibid.*, p. 339.
50. Charanis, *op. cit.*, p. 187.
51. Cahen, *op. cit.*, p. 29.
52. Lopez, *op. cit.*, pp. 64-65.

53. Kordatos, *op. cit.*, p. 501.
54. Hussey, *op. cit.*, p. 210.
55. Khuda Bukhsh, *op. cit.*, p. 204.
56. The contract between Michael VII and Robert Guiscard be-trothing Constantine to Helen may be found in Bezobrazov, *Russian Journ. Min. Instr. Publ.*, 1889, Vol. 265, apud Buckler, *op. cit.*, p. 314, n. 2.
57. Charanis, *op. cit.*, pp. 187-88.
58. Psellos, "Michael VII," *op. cit.*, n. 1, pp. 369-70.
59. *Logothete*—in charge of financial accounts, a chancellor, Psellos, *op. cit.*, Glossary p. 388.
60. Psellos, *op. cit.*, p. 370, n. 1.
61. Peter Charanis, "Byzantium, the West and the Origin of the First Crusade," in *Byzantion* XIX (1949), pp. 22, 23, 24.
62. Grégoire, *op. cit.* (1957), III, 24, p. 899.
63. F. Chalandon, *Essai sur le régne d'Alexis Ier Comnène, 1081-1118* (Paris, 1900), p. 12.
64. Cahen, *op. cit.*, p. 76.
65. Dyrrachium was a key city of the Byzantine Empire and the object of several sieges in the course of the account in the *Alexiad*. Buckler points out that Anna has devoted twenty-two chapters wholly or in part to Dyrrachium: III, 12; IV, 1-8; V, 1; VI, 6; XII, 9; XIII, 2-11. Buckler, *op cit.*, p. 398 and 398, n. 2.
66. "Immortals"—army of scattered soldiers originally from Asia; they had cuirass, helmets, buckler, and lances; they were created by Michael VII Ducas. Grégoire, *op. cit.*, IV, 4, pp. 904-5. Anna calls them "the most select regiment of the Roman army" (II, 9, p. 63).
67. Celtic troops—Franks of Italy. Grégoire, *op. cit.*, IV, 4, p. 904.
68. N. H. Baynes and H. St. L. B. Moss, *Byzantium* (Oxford, 1962), p. 28.
69. Peter Charanis, "The Byzantine Empire in the Eleventh Century," p. 189, in *A History of the Crusades*, ed. K. M. Setton (Philadelphia, 1955), pp. 177-219.
70. Diehl, *op. cit.*, p. 106.
71. Chalandon, *op. cit.*, p. 37.
72. *Ibid.*, p. 38.
73. Stanescu, *op. cit.*, p. 407.
74. Chalandon, *op. cit.*, p. 12.

Chapter Two

1. Karl Hopf, *Griechenland, Separatausgabe aus der Allgem. Engyklopedia von Ersch and Gruber*, VI (Leipzig, 1870), p. 165; apud G. Murnu, "L'Origine des Comnènes," p. 213, in *Academia*

Română, Sectiunes Istorica Bulletin, Vol. XI (Bucharest, 1924), pp. 212-16.

2. The Vlachs are those nomads of the Balkan peninsula who, in the present day Rumanians still claim to be Romans in race, language and descent. Buckler, *op. cit.,* p. 265 and references.

3. M. Gyoni, "Le Nom de Blachoi dans l'*Alexiade* d'Anne Comnène," in *B. Z.* (Munich, 1951), p. 244.

4. Chalandon, *op. cit.,* p. 21.

5. Lysimaque Oeconomos, *La Vie Religieuse dans l'Empire byzantin au temps des Comnènes et des Anges* (Paris, 1918), p. 11.

6. George Finlay, *A History of Greece* (Oxford, 1877), Vol. III, p. 8, n. 1.

7. Grégoire, *op. cit.* (1953), II, 1, p. 476.

8. *Ibid.*

9. Psellos, *op. cit.,* p. 276, n. 3.

10. Grégoire, *op. cit.,* I, 2, p. 477.

11. Chalandon, *op. cit.,* p. 22.

12. Hussey, *op. cit.,* p. 205.

13. Vryonis, *op. cit.,* p. 309.

14. Hussey, *op. cit.,* p. 205.

15. Psellos, *op. cit.,* p. 315, n. 1.

16. Hussey, *op. cit.,* p. 206.

17. Psellos, *op. cit.,* p. 316.

18. *Ibid.,* p. 307.

19. A. A. Vasiliev, *History of the Byzantine Empire, 324-1453,* second English edition revised (Madison, Wisconsin, 1952), pp. 355, 358.

20. Hussey, *op. cit.,* p. 206.

21. Psellos, *op. cit.,* p. 311.

22. Finlay, *op. cit.,* III, p. 9.

23. Psellos, *op. cit.,* pp. 311, 312, 313, 314.

24. *Protovestiarios*—in charge of the emperor's wardrobe and the monies concerned with it. Psellos, *op. cit.,* Glossary p. 388.

25. *Curopalates*—"major-domo of the imperial palace," as defined by E. A. Sophocles in *Greek Lexicon of the Roman and Byzantine Periods;* normally conferred on members of the Imperial family. Psellos, *op. cit.,* Glossary p. 388.

26. Scylitzes 813, p. 650, apud Psellos, *op. cit.,* p. 304, n. 1.

27. Finlay, *op. cit.,* pp. 11-12.

28. Grégoire, *op. cit.,* I, 4, p. 478.

29. Psellos, *op. cit.,* p. 329.

30. Ostrogorsky, *op. cit.,* p. 301.

31. Chalandon, *op. cit.,* p. 23.

32. Finlay, *op. cit.,* p. 12-13.

33. Grégoire, *op. cit.,* I, 6, p. 480. In an article by Peter Charanis,

the author states that "Nicephoros Melissanos, according to the French translation of Bryennios by Henri Grégoire, is said to have been related to the Bourtzos family on his father's side. This would indicate that the Melissenoi were of Armenian origin." Grégoire, *op. cit.*, p. 480. However, Charanis also points out that "the Bonn edition of Bryennios (p. 24) has Mortious not Bourtzos." Peter Charanis, *The Armenians in the Byzantine Empire* (Calouste Gulbenkian Foundation, Armenian Library) (Lisboa, 1963), p. 46, n. 173.

34. *Ibid.*, p. 46, n. 171.

35. Steven Runciman, "Education and Learning," *Byzantine Civilization* (London, 1933), Chapter 9, pp. 223-39.

36. *Paideia Basiliki*, p. 257 and 265, apud Chalandon, *op. cit.*, p. 24, n. 3 and p. 25.

37. Grégoire, *op. cit.*, I, 6, p. 481.

38. *Ibid.*, I, 6, p. 480.

39. Chalandon, *op. cit.*, p. 26.

40. Grégoire, *op. cit.*, I, 6, p. 480.

41. *Protostrator*—first of the cavalry grooms of the Byzantine Imperial court. *Panlexikon*, ed. G. Dragatakis (Athens, 1959), Vol. 5, p. 3855.

42. Grégoire, *op. cit.*, I, 12, pp. 486-87.

43. *Ibid.*, I, 22, p. 497.

44. Ioannes Zonaras, *Epitome Historiarum* (Leipzig, 1868-75), Vol. 4, XVIII, 21, p. 235.

45. V. Laurent, "Une Titulature abusive: Anne Ière Dalassène," in *Academia Română Sectiunes Istorica Bulletin* (Bucharest, 1946), Vol. XXVII, pp. 33-41.

46. *Ibid.*

47. Zonaras, *op. cit.*, 4, XVIII, 21, p. 235.

48. Laurent, *op. cit.*, p. 38.

49. The date 1105 is not precise and can vary by a number of years. Chalandon, *op. cit.*, p. 273.

50. Grégoire, *op. cit.*, II, 3, p. 503.

51. *Ibid.*, I, 6, p. 480.

52. The archbishop who had denounced the plot was Theophylactos, Archbishop of Achrida in Bulgaria. Bernard Leib, *Alexiade* (Paris, 1937-45), Vol. 2, p. 148, n. 1.

53. Grégoire, *op. cit.*, II, 4, 5, 6, 7, 8, pp. 504-8.

54. Demetrios I. Polemis, *The Doukai* (London, 1968), p. 10.

55. Grégoire, *op. cit.*, Preface, pp. 473-74.

56. *Ibid.* (1957), III, 6, p. 886.

57. Polemis, *op. cit.*, p. 58 and references.

58. Grégoire, *op. cit.* (1953), I, 16, p. 491.

59. Polemis, *op. cit.*, p. 56.

60. Psellos, *op. cit.*, p. 375, n. 1.

61. Bryennios, p. 12, apud Polemis, *op. cit.*, p. 62 and 62, n. 8.

62. Buckler, *op. cit.*, p. 159 and references; also p. 134, n. 6.

63. Zonaras, *op. cit.*, 4, XVIII, 21, p. 236.

64. Polemis, *op. cit.*, p. 41 and references.

65. Buckler, *op. cit.*, p. 125.

66. Polemis, *op. cit.*, p. 44 and references.

67. Grégoire, *op. cit.* (1957), III, 6, p. 886.

68. Demetrios Polemis, "Notes on Eleventh Century Chronology," in *B. Z.* 58 (1965), pp. 68-69.

69. *Nemitzi*—Germans whom Anna describes as the ax-bearing barbarians. These were a barbaric tribe who were the subjects of the Roman Empire of old. *Alexiad*, II, 9, 64.

70. Demetrios Polemis, *The Doukai* (London, 1968), p. 70.

71. *Ibid.*

72. Grégoire, *op. cit.* (1953), "Preface," p. 475.

73. Zonaras, *op. cit.*, 4, XVIII, 29, p. 259.

74. Theodore Prodromos, in Ed. Kurtz, "Unedierte Texte," *B. Z.* 16 (Leipzig, 1907), p. 88.

75. Acominatos (Nicetas) Chionates, "Preface" *History of John Comnenos*, unpublished translation by Procope S. Costas, pp. 6-7.

76. "Typikon," in (Migne's) *Patrologia Graeca* (Paris, 1864), Vol. 127, cols. 985-1120.

77. *Ibid.*, col. 1081.

78. *Ibid.*, col. 1092.

79. Ed. Kurtz, "Das Todesjahr der Kaiserin Irene," in "Unedierte Texte," *B. Z.* XVI (Leipzig, 1907), p. 74.

80. Jean Darrouzès, "Discours Sur La Mort de la Porphyrogenétè Kyra Anna La Kaissarissa" in *Georges et Demetrios Tornikes Lettres et Discours* (Paris, 1970), p. 247.

81. William of Tyre, XV, 23, apud Buckler, *op. cit.*, p. 249, n. 5.

Chapter Three

1. "Quaternion"—the quaternion of learning had two divisions: the quadrivium and the trivium. In medieval universities, the quadrivium embraced geometry, astronomy, arithmetic and music; the trivium embraced grammar, logic and rhetoric; both of these formed the three years' course between the taking of the B. A. and the M. A. *New Standard Dictionary*, Funk and Wagnalls, pp. 2023 and 2569.

2. Prodromos, "Poem on the Death of Theodora," in Ed. Kurtz, "Unedierte Texte," *B. Z.* XVI (Leipzig, 1907), p. 88, lines 43-45.

3. Prodromos, "Epithalamium" in (Migne's) *P. G.* (Paris, 1864), Vol. 133, col. 1401.

4. Zonaras, *op. cit.*, Vol. 4, XVIII, p. 251.

5. Costas, *op. cit.*, p. 12.

6. Darrouzès, *op. cit.*, p. 231.
7. Demetrios Dematrakos, *Mega Lexikon Ellinikis Glossis* (Athens, 1959), Vol. 8, p. 7053.
8. Runciman, *op. cit.*, p. 230.
9. Darrouzès, *op. cit.*, p. 243.
10. *Ibid.*, p. 263.
11. Buckler, *op. cit.*, pp. 175, 197.
12. Radoslav Katičič, "I Archaiomatheia kai to Epikon Pnevma eis tin *Alexiada* tis Annis tis Komninis," in *Epetiris Etaireias Byzantinon Spoudon* (Athens, 1959), Vol. 29, pp. 81-86.
13. Darrouzès, *op. cit.*, pp. 285-93.
14. Buckler, *op. cit.*, p. 194.
15. Nicetas Chionates states that Alexios is made to call his son-in-law rather scornfully a Macedonian. Costas, *op. cit.*, p. 6.
16. Kurtz, *op. cit.*, p. 100.
17. J. Segar, "Nikephoros Bryennios," in *Byz. Hist. der 10ten u. 11ten Jahrh. I*, pp. 14-17, apud Buckler, *op. cit.*, p. 33 and 33, n. 3.
18. Zonaras, *op. cit.*, 4, XVIII, 22, p. 240.
19. Grégoire, *op. cit.*, "La Famille Bryenne," pp. 466-68.
20. *Ibid.*
21. Grégoire, *op. cit.*, "Preface," p. 475.
22. Zonaras, *op. cit.*, 4, XVIII, 24, pp. 246-47.
23. Costas, *op. cit.*, p. 5.
24. Prodromos (Migne's), *P. G.* Vol. 133, col. 1399.
25. Kurtz, *op. cit.*, p. 100.
26. "Typikon," *op. cit.*, Vol. 127, col. 1116.
27. Prodromos, "On the Death of Theodora," in Kurtz, *op. cit.*, pp. 87-93.
28. Zonaras, *op. cit.*, 4, XVIII, 28, p. 256.

Chapter Four

1. Frederick Chalandon, *Jean Comnène 1118-1143 et Manuel Comnène 1143-1180* (Paris, 1912), Vol. I, p. 5.
2. Costas, *op. cit.*, pp. 5-6.
3. *Ibid.*, p. 9.
4. Th. I. Uspensky, "The Constantinopolitan Code of Seraglio," *Transactions of the Russian Archaeological Institute at Constantinople* XII (1907), 30-31, apud Vasiliev, *op. cit.*, p. 490 and 490, n. 352.
5. Theodore Prodromos, "Os Apo tou Porphyrogenitou Kyrou Isaakiou tou Komnenou," in Kurtz, *op. cit.*, pp. 107-8.
6. Buckler, *op. cit.*, p. 9 and p. 9, nn. 5, 6, 7; also cf. Kurtz, *op. cit.*, pp. 104ff.
7. Zonaras, *op. cit.*, 4, XVIII, 22, p. 241.
8. Rosprawy Akad. Umiejet wydzial filol. (Krakow) Ser. II, XXI, 1903, p. 360, apud Buckler, *op. cit.*, pp. 5-6 and p. 6, n. 1.

9. Zonaras, *op. cit.*, 4, XVIII, 22, p. 241.

10. F. Chalandon, *Essai sur le Règne d'Alexis Ier Comnène, 1081-1118* (Paris, 1900), pp. 275-76.

11. Costas, *op. cit.*, pp. 6-7.

12. *Ibid.*, pp. 7-8.

13. Zonaras, *op. cit.*, 4, XVIII, 28, p. 257.

14. Costas, *op. cit.*, p. 9.

15. *Ibid.*, p. 8.

16. *Ibid.*, p. 9.

17. *Ibid.*, p. 12.

18. *Ibid.*

19. Acominatos (Nicetas) Chionates, *Historia*, ed. Bekker, *Corpus Scriptorum Historiae Byzantinae* pars. 14 (Bonn, 1835), pp. 63-64.

20. Runciman, *op. cit.*, p. 106.

21. Chionates, *op. cit.*, p. 23.

22. Dölger, Reg. 1312 apud Ostrogorsky, *op. cit.*, p. 337 and p. 337, n. 1.

23. Vasiliev, *op. cit.*, p. 415.

24. F. Chalandon, *Jean Comnène 1118-1143 et Manuel Comnène 1143-1180* (Paris, 1912), Vol. I, pp. 32-34.

25. *Ibid.*, p. 11.

26. *Ibid.*, pp. 16-17.

27. Darrouzès, *op. cit.*, p. 282.

28. *Ibid.*

Chapter Five

1. *Domestic of the Schools*—man of confidence of his "patron." E. Hanton, "Lexique explicatif du Recueil des inscriptions grecques chrétiennes d'Asie Mineure," p. 77 in *Byzantion* IV (1927-28), pp. 53-136. This is one of the most important functions of the empire.

2. Anna is in agreement with her husband who blames Borilos, the favorite of Botaneiates, for having blinded the prisoner without the knowledge of Alexios. Grégoire, *op. cit.* (1957), IV, 17, p. 914.

3. Basilacios had the troops of Illyria, the troops charged to guard Bulgaria, and the Varangians that Michael VII had given him when he sent him to Dyrrachium as Duke to replace Nicephoros Bryennios who had revolted. *Ibid.*, IV, 26, p. 913.

4. *Ibid.*, IV, 27, p. 919.

5. *Quinquagesima*—the time from the Sunday before Lent to Easter Sunday, or the first week of this time. *Webster's International Dictionary*, second edition (1934), p. 2043.

6. *Hagia Sophia*, also known as Saint Sophia, was first built under Constantine I; it was rebuilt by Justinian on the site of the small basilica of Saint Sophia ("divine wisdom") after the sedition of Nika

(532) during which it was burned. It was inaugurated on December 27, 537. A. A. Vasiliev, *History of the Byzantine Empire 324-1453*, second edition in English, revised (Madison, Wisconsin, 1952), p. 188.

Chapter Six

1. Ostrogorsky, *op. cit.*, p. 317.
2. Chalandon, *Essai sur le Règne d'Alexis I*er *Comnène, 1081-1118* (Paris, 1900), p. 80.
3. Horatio F. Brown, "The Venetians and the Venetian Quarter to the Close of the Twelfth Century," in *The Journal of Hellenic Studies* (London, 1920), XL: 68-88.
4. Vasiliev, *op. cit.*, p. 413.
5. Hussey, *op. cit.*, p. 218.
6. George Ostrogorsky, *History of the Byzantine Empire* (Oxford, 1969), p. 371.
7. *Ibid.*, pp. 371-72; also Vasiliev, *op. cit.*, p. 480.
8. Vasiliev, *op. cit.*, pp. 479, 480.
9. *Ibid.*, p. 480.
10. *Ibid.*, pp. 471-72.
11. Oman, *op. cit.*, p. 257.
12. Buckler, *op. cit.*, p. 231.
13. Claude Cahen, *Pre-Ottoman Turkey* (New York, 1968), p. 77.
14. Leib states that Anna confuses the names of sultans. She calls Kilij Arslan (Clitziasthlan). She gives the son the name of the father (Clitziasthlan) Shahinshah (the Saisan of a little later) or Malik Shah (the name in her history are one and the same person). Leib, *op. cit.*, III, p. 188, n. 1.
15. Chalandon identifies the eclipse as that of August 1, 1087. Chalandon, *op. cit.*, p. 106, n. 2.
16. *Pallium*—a relic of the Virgin, a short cape preserved in the Church of the Blachernae and carried at times in their campaigns by the basileus. Leib observes that the fact that Alexios must abandon the omophorion of the Virgin Mary shows the extent of the defeat. Leib, *op. cit.*, II, p. 108, n. 6.
17. Leib quotes Plutarch, *Pelop.* 18, and states that the Sacred Band was invented by the Thebans against the Lacadaemonians. Leib, *op. cit.*, II, p. 108, n. 6.
18. Vasilievsky, "Byzantium and the Patzinaks," *Works*, Vol. I, p. 107, apud Vasiliev, *op. cit.*, p. 385 and p. 385, n. 29.
19. Chalandon, *op. cit.*, "Introduction," pp. xii-xiii.
20. *Saniscus*: As Leib suggests, this may be an error of the copyist; it may be *neaniskos*—"the young"—and since Anna erroneously calls Bohemond the youngest son of Guiscard, the Normans ascertain that although Bohemond is the oldest, he was not the heir of his father's power. The common people went by appearances and the surname

neaniskos stayed with him. Leib, *op. cit.*, II, "Notes Complimentaires," p. 238.

21. Alexios sent the letters first to Hermann, duke of Longobardia (nephew of Robert) against whom he revolted in 1078 with his brother Abelard. Chalandon, *op. cit.*, pp. 67-68.

22. According to Leib, Alexios left Isaac in the capital to maintain order because there was then in Constantinople a party of malcontents, and Alexios had to be on guard against their attempts to revolt. His brother Isaac, the Sebastocrator, had to repress all disorder while his mother would govern by virtue of the Chrysobull. Leib, *op. cit.*, I, p. 150, n. 2.

23. Oman, *op. cit.*, pp. 260-61.

24. Vasiliev, *op. cit.*, p. 381.

25. Chalandon, *op. cit.*, p. 94.

26. Peter Charanis, "Aims of the Medieval Crusades and How They Are Viewed by Byzantium," p. 125, in *Church History*, 21 (1952), pp. 123-35.

27. Steven Runciman, *A History of the Crusades* (Cambridge, 1968), Vol. I, p. 103.

28. Ostrogorsky, *op. cit.*, p. 321.

29. Hussey, *op. cit.*, p. 214.

30. Runciman, *op. cit.*, pp. 115-16.

31. Chalandon, *op. cit.*, pp. 155-58.

32. Vasiliev, *op. cit.*, p. 402.

33. Charanis, *op. cit.*, p. 126.

34. *Ibid.*

35. *Ibid.*

36. *Ibid.*

37. *Ibid.*

38. D. C. Munro, "Did the Emperor Alexios I Ask for Aid at the Council of Piacenza, 1095?" in *American Historical Review*, 27, No. 4 (July, 1922), pp. 1-5.

39. Charanis, *op. cit.*, pp. 125, 126, 128.

40. Runciman, *op. cit.*, "Appendix II," p. 337 and p. 169.

41. Chalandon, *op. cit.*, p. 169.

42. August C. Krey, *The First Crusade* (London, 1921), p. 71.

43. Anna calls the sacred object a "nail," Latin chroniclers call it a "Lance." Cf. Buckler, *op. cit.*, pp. 467-68.

44. Oman, *op. cit.*, pp. 263-64.

45. Krey, *op. cit.*, pp. 82, 83.

46. *Ibid.*, p. 93.

47. Chalandon, *op. cit.*, p. 252.

48. Karl Krumbacher, *Geschichte der byzantinischen Litteratur, von Justinian bis zum Ende des Oströmischen Reichas (527-1453)*,

in *Handbuch der Altertums Wissenschaft,* Abt 9, Teil 1 (Munich, 1897), p. 275.

49. Speros Vryonis, Jr., *Byzantium and Europe* (New York, 1967), p. 149.

50. Chalandon, *op. cit.,* p. 90.

51. Oman, *op. cit.,* p. 267.

52. Buckler, *op. cit.,* p. 470.

53. *Ibid.,* p. 231, n. 8.

54. Oeconomos, *op. cit.,* p. 48.

55. *Ibid.,* p. 17.

56. Peter Charanis, "The Byzantine Empire in the Eleventh Century," p. 215, in *A History of the Crusades,* ed. K. M. Setton (Madison, Wisconsin, 1969), second edition, pp. 177-219.

57. Joan Hussey, *Church and Learning in the Byzantine Empire, 867-1185* (New York, 1963), p. 95 and p. 95, n. 1.

58. *Ibid.*

59. Chalandon, *op. cit.,* p. 91.

60. According to the official acts of the "Trial" published by Th. Uspensky (in the *Bulletin de l'Institut Archéologique russe de Constantinople* [1897], Vol. II, pp. 1-66, Greek text and study in Russian), the date is given as 1082 (February, March, April). The report was done in the winter which followed the defeat of Alexios at Dyrrachium, apud Leib, *op. cit.,* Vol. II, pp. 32-33, n. 2.

61. Hussey, *op. cit.,* pp. 93-94.

62. Acominatos (Nicetas) Chionates, *Thesavros Orthodoxia,* ed. Tafel, p. 1 and ff., apud Chalandon, *op. cit.,* p. 312.

63. During the trial one. of the disciples of Italos protested that he had not learned any heretical doctrines from his master but only the art of speaking well. Leib, *op. cit.,* II, "Notes Complimentaires," p. 239.

64. Hussey, *op. cit.,* p. 92.

65. *Ibid.*

66. *Ibid.,* p. 94.

67. Chalandon, *op. cit.,* p. 314.

Chapter Seven

1. Buckler, *op. cit.,* p. 231.

2. Chalandon, *op. cit.,* p. 100.

3. *Ibid.,* p. 323.

4. Vryonis, *op. cit.,* p. 141.

5. F. J. Foakes-Jackson, "Anna Comnena," *Hibbert Journal,* XXXIII (1934-35), p. 430.

6. Speros Vryonis, Jr., "Byzantine *Demokratia* and the Guilds in the 11th Century," *Dumbarton Oaks Papers* No. 17 (Washington, 1963), p. 310.

7. Georgina Buckler, "Women in Byzantine Law About 1100 A. D.," in *Byzantion* XI (1936), Fasc. 2, pp. 391-416.

8. *Mousai Alexiades Komniniades,* ed. P. Maas, *B. Z.* XXII (1913), pp. 348-62.

9. Vasiliev, *op. cit.,* pp. 488-89.

10. Zonaras, *op. cit.,* 4, XVIII, 24, p. 244.

11. Chalandon, *op. cit.,* p. 323.

12. Krumbacher, *op. cit.,* p. 276.

13. Buckler, *op. cit.,* p. 231.

14. Charles Diehl, *La Société byzantine à l'Époque des Comnène* (Paris, 1929), p. 8.

15. Zonaras, *op. cit.,* 4, XXVIII, 26, p. 251.

16. Sophia Antoniades, "Neoellinika Stoicheia sta Epta Biblia tis *Alexiados,*" in *Eis Mnimin Spiridonos Lambrou* (Athens, 1935), p. 371.

17. Gyula Moravczik, "Byzantinoturcica I," *Die Byzantinischen Quellen der Geschichte der Türkvölker.* Akademie Verlag (Berlin, 1958), p. 220.

18. Hariton Haritonides, "Paratereseis Kritikai kai Grammatikai eis Annan Komnene," in *Academia Athenon Pragmateia tis Akademias Athenon,* Vol. 15 (Athens, 1949, 1951), p. 40.

19. Buckler, *op. cit.,* p. 495; Antoniades, *op. cit.,* p. 373.

20. Antoniades, *op. cit.,* p. 371.

21. Buckler, *op. cit.,* p. 495; Antoniades, *op. cit.,* p. 373.

22. Krumbacher, *op. cit.,* p. 277.

23. R. M. Dawkins "The Greek Language in the Byzantine Period," p. 253, in Baynes and Moss, *op. cit.,* pp. 252-67.

24. N. Iorga, "Medallions d'histoire littéraire byzantine 18 Anne Comnène," in *Byzantion* 2 (1925), p. 283.

Selected Bibliography

1. *Books in English:*

BAYNES, N. H. *The Byzantine Empire*. London, 1925.

BAYNES, N. H. and Moss, H. St. L. B. *Byzantium*. Oxford, 1962.

BROWN, HORATIO F. "The Venetians and the Venetian Quarter in Constantinople to the Close of the 12th Century." *Journal of Hellenic Studies*, 40 (1920), 68-88.

BROWNING, ROBERT. "An Unpublished Funeral Oration of Anna Comnena" (English text). *Proceedings of the Cambridge Philological Society*, No. 188, new series No. 8 (1962), 1-12.

BUCKLER, GEORGINA. *Anna Comnena*. Oxford, 1968.

—————. "Women in Byzantine Law About 1100 A. D." *Byzantion* XI, 2 (1936), 391-416.

—————. "Byzantine Education." In *Byzantium* by N. H. Baynes and H. St. L. B. Moss (Oxford, 1962), 200-220.

CAHEN, CLAUDE. *Pre-Ottoman Turkey*. Translated from the French by J. Jones-Williams. London, 1968.

—————. "The Turkish Invasion: The Selchukids." *A History of the Crusades*, ed. K. M. Setton. Vol. I. (Philadelphia, 1955), 135-76, and second edition (Madison, Wisconsin, 1969).

CHARANIS, PETER. "Aims of the Medieval Crusades and How They Are Viewed by Byzantium." *Church History* 21 (1952), 123-25. 123-25.

—————. *The Armenians in the Byzantine Empire* (Calouste Gulbenkian Foundation, Armenian Library) (Lisboa, 1963), 12-63.

—————. "The Byzantine Empire in the 11th Century." *A History of the Crusades*, ed. K. M. Setton, Vol. I (Philadelphia, 1955) 177-219, and second edition (Madison, Wisconsin, 1969).

—————. "Byzantium, the West and the Origin of the First Crusade." *Byzantion*, XIX (1949), 17-24.

COSTAS, PROCOPE S. "Preface." Acominatos (Nicetas) Chionates. *Historia*, ed. Bekker, *Corpus Scriptorum Historiae Byzantinae* pars. 14 (Bonn, 1835), "Preface," pp. 1-12 (unpublished translation).

DAWES, E. A. S. *The Alexiad*. London, 1967.

173

DAWKINS, R. M. "The Greek Language in the Byzantine Period." In *Byzantium* by N. H. Baynes and H. St. L. B. Moss (Oxford, 1962), 252-67.

DIEHL, CHARLES. *History of the Byzantine Empire.* New York, 1967.

FINLAY, GEORGE. *A History of Greece.* Vol. 3, Oxford, 1877.

HUSSEY, JOAN M. "Byzantium and its Neighbors." *The Cambridge Medieval History,* Vol. IV, pt. 1 (Cambridge, 1967), 205-45.

————. *The Byzantine World* (second edition). London, 1961.

————. "The Byzantine Empire in the Eleventh Century: Some Different Interpretations." In *Transactions of the Royal Historical Society.* Fourth Series, Vol. XXXII (London, 1950), 71-85.

————. *Church and Learning in the Byzantine Empire.* New York, 1963.

JENKINS, R. J. H. "Social Life in the Byzantine Empire." *The Cambridge Medieval History.* Vol. IV, pt. 2 (Cambridge, 1967), 80-103.

S. KHUDA BUKHSH. *Contributions to the History of Islamic Civilization.* Calcutta, 1905.

KREY, A. C. *The First Crusade.* Princeton, 1921.

LOPEZ, RORERT S. "The Norman Conquest of Sicily." *A History of the Crusades,* ed. K. M. Setton, Vol. I (Philadelphia, 1955), 54-67.

MUNRO, D. C. "Did the Emperor Alexios Ask for Aid at the Council of Piacenza in 1095?" *American Historical Review* 27, no. 4 (July, 1922), 1-5.

OMAN, SIR CHARLES. *Story of the Byzantine Empire.* London, 1892.

————. *The History of the Art of War in the Middle Ages* (second edition). London, 1924.

OSTROGORSKY, GEORGE. *History of the Byzantine State.* Translated by Joan M. Hussey. New Brunswick, 1957; also Oxford, 1969.

POLEMIS, DEMETRIOS. "Notes on Eleventh Century Chronology." *B. Z.* 58 (1965), 68-69.

————. *The Doukai.* University of London, 1968.

PSELLOS, MICHAEL. *Fourteen Byzantine Rulers, the Chronographia.* Translated by E. R. A. Sewter. London, 1953.

RUNCIMAN, STEVEN. *A History of the Crusades,* Vol. I, Cambridge, 1957.

————. *Byzantine Civilization.* London, 1933.

VASILIEV, A. A. *History of the Byzantine Empire, 324-1453* (second English edition, revised). Madison, Wisconsin, 1952.

VRYONIS, SPEROS, JR., "Byzantium: The Social Basis of Decline in the 11th Century." *Greek, Roman and Byzantine Studies,* II (1959), 151-75.

————. *Byzantium and Europe,* New York, 1967.

————. "Byzantine *Demokratia* and the Guilds in the 11th Century." *Dumbarton Oaks Papers*, No. 17 (Washington, 1963), 289-314.

2. *Books in French*:

CHALANDON, FREDERICK. *Essai sur le règne d'Alexis Ier Comnène, 1081-1118*. Paris, 1900.

————. *Jean Comnène 1118-1143 et Manuel Ier Comnène, 1143-1180*. Vol. I (Paris, 1912).

————. *Histoire de la Domination Normande en Italie et en Sicile*. Vol. I (Paris, 1907).

DARROUZÈS, JEAN. "Discours sur la Mort de la Porphyrogenétè Kyra Anna La Kaisarissa," in *Georges et Demetrios Tornikes Lettres et Discours* (Paris, 1970), pp. 220-323.

DIEHL, CHARLES. *La société byzantine à l'Époque des Comnène* Paris, 1929.

————. *Mélanges Charles Diehl*, Vol. I (Paris, 1930).

GRÉGOIRE, HENRI. "Les Quatres Livres des Histoires," *Byzantion 23* (1952-53), 469-530; *Byzantion 25-27* (1957), 881-926.

GYONI, MATYAS. "Le Nom de Blachi dans l'*Alexiade* d'Anne Comnène," *B. Z. 44* (1951), 241-52.

HAGENMEYER, H. *Chronologie de la Première Croisade (1094-1100)*. Paris, 1902.

HANTON, E. "Lexique explicatif du Recueil des inscriptions grecques chrétiennes d'Asie Mineure." *Byzantion IV* (1927-28), 53-136.

IORGA, N. "Medallions d'histoire littéraire byzantine 18 Anne Comnène." *Byzantion 2* (1925), 281-283.

LAURENT, V. "Une titulare abusive: Anne Ière Delassene." *Academie Românǎ Sectiunea Istorica Bulletin* (1946), Vol. 27, 33-41.

LEIB, BERNARD. *Alexiade* 3 vols. Paris, 1937-45.

————. "Contributions à l'étude des manuscrits et du texte de l'*Alexiade* d'Anne Comnène." *Mélanges Charles Diehl*, I (Paris, 1930), 191-99.

MURNU, G. "L'Origine des Comnènes." *Academia Românǎ Sectiunes Istorica.* Bulletin 11 (1924), 212-16.

OECONOMOS, LYSIMAQUE. *La Vie Religieuse dans l'Empire byzantin au temps des Comnènes et des Anges*. Paris, 1918.

SCHLUMBERGER, GUSTAVE. "Sceaux Byzantins Inédits," in *Revue des Études Grecques VII* (1894), pp. 319-36.

STANESCU, EUGEN. "Un Quart de siècles de reformes et contreréformes impériales (1057-1081)." *Proceedings of the XIIIth International Congress of Byzantine Studies* Oxford 5-10, September, 1966 (London, 1967), 401-8.

176   ANNA COMNENA

3. *Books in Greek:*
P. G. = (Migne's) *Patrologia Graeca.* Vols. 127, 133.

ACOMINATOS (NICETAS) CHIONATES. *Historia,* ed. Bekker, *Corpus Scriptorum Historiae Byzantinae* pars. 14 (Bonn, 1835).

ANTONIADI, SOPHIA. "Neoellinika Stoicheia sta Epta Biblia tis *Alexiados.*" *Eis Mnimin Spyridonos Lambrou* (Athens, 1935), 370-74.

————. "Perigraphiki stin *Alexiada* pos I Anne Comnini Elepi kai Zographizi Prosopa kai haraktires." *Ellinika* 5 (1932), 255-76.

BRYENNIOS, NICEPHOROS. "Hyle Historias." (Migne's) *Patrologia Graeca* (Paris, 1864), Vol. 127, 23-217.

COMNÈNE, ANNE. *Alexias* (Greek text). Bernard Leib, *Alexiade,* 3 vols. Paris, 1937-45.

————. "Prologue to her Will." Ed. Kurtz, *B. Z.* XVI (Leipzig, 1907), 98-101.

DEMETRAKOS, DEMETRIOS. *Mega Lexikon Ellinikis Glossis.* Athens, 1959.

HARITONIDES, HARITON. "Paratereseis Kritikai kai Grammatikai eis Annan Komnene." *Akademie Athenon- Pragmateia Tis Akademias Athenon.* Vol. 14 (Athens, 1949, 1951), 1-46.

KATIČIČ, RADOSLAV. "I Archaeomatheia kai to Epikon Pnevma eis tin *Alexiada* tis Annas tis Komnenes." *Epetiris Etaireias Byzantinon Spoudon.* Vol. 29 (Athens, 1959), 81-86.

Megali Helleniki Engyklopedia, ed. Pavlos Drandaki. Athens (second edition), *Byzantion,* Vol. 7.

PRODROMOS, THEODORE. "Os Apo Tou Porphyrogenitou Kyrou Isaakou tou Komnenou." Ed. Kurtz, "Unedierte Texte," *B. Z.* XVI (Leipzig, 1907), 107-8.

————. "The Death of Theodora," *B. Z.* XVI (Leipzig, 1907), 87-93.

————. "Epithalamium. *P. G.* Vol. 133, cols. 1399, 1401.

TORNIKES, GEORGIOS. "Logos epi to thanato tis Porphyrogenitou Kyras Annes tis Kaisarissis," in Jean Darrouzès, *Georges et Demetrios Tornikes Lettres et Discours* (Paris, 1970), 220-323.

Typikon. P. G. 127, cols. 984-1127.

ZONARAS, IOANNES. *Epitome Historiarum* (Leipzig, 1868-75), Vol. 4.

4. *Books in German:*
B. Z. = Byzantinische Zeitschrift.

KRUMBACHER, KARL. *Geschichte der Byzantinischen Litteratur von Justinian bus zum Ende des Oströmischen Reiches (527-1453)* (*Handbuch der Altertums-Wissenschaft,* Abt 9, Teil 1) (Munich, 1897), 273-76 (2nd. ed.).

KURTZ, ED. "Das Testament der Anna Komnena." *B. Z.* XVI (Leipzig, 1907), 93-101.

————. "Das Todesjahr der Kaiserin Irene." *B. Z.* (Leipzig, 1907), 69-75.

MORAVCSIK, GYULA. *Byzantinoturcica I Die byzantinischen Quellen der Geschichte der Türkvölker.* Akademie Verlag (Berlin, 1958), 219-23 (2nd. ed.).

OSTER, K. *Anna Komnena.* Restatt, 1868-71.

5. *Book in Latin:*

FUESLINI, JOH. CONRADI. *Dissertatio de Alexiade Annae Comnenae.* Thuringia, 1766.

Index

179

182 ANNA COMNENA